The Quiet Revolution Of the Heart

A New Renaissance

Rebecca Cherry

First Edition, June 2018

For information contact:

Isabella's Earth LLC

484 White Cap Lane

Newport Coast, CA 92657

E: rcherry@rebecca-cherry.com

Published in the United States by Isabella's Earth Publishing, a division of Isabella's Earth LLC

ISBN:
ISBN-13: 978-1985171589

DEDICATION

This book is dedicated to the Divine Feminine in all of us.

She is strong yet serene.
She is vulnerable yet confident to the winds of change coming.
She is Beauty beyond words.
She is compassion.
She is Love.
She is the Mother's warmth.
She is the quiet strength that emboldens you through the storm.
She simply is.
She is me.
She is you.
She is the Divine Feminine in all of us.
Remember her. Awaken to her. Embody her.
Now be her.
For you.
For me.
For all of us.

ACKNOWLEDGMENTS

There are always people in your life that stand out. They unequivocally support you. They definitely love you. And although they may not always understand you, they still have your back.

This is a special type of person who leaves judgment at the door of their hearts. They know that their love for you rises above any doubt, petty frustration or momentary anger.

This type of person will be there when things crumble around you. They will extend a hand and help you rebuild and rise from the ashes of your life with grace and love.

They listen when you are at the end of your rope and respond with encouraging words and more love.

They believe in you. They believe in your dreams. Even when you are deep in self-doubt.

They ascribe no timeline of expectations or reward.
No strings are attached for the day of recompense.

They give for one reason alone.
Love.

I am truly blessed to have a few of these people in my life. And without them I would not be writing this now.

To my beautiful son and compatriot in life, Gianni:
I love you more than life itself. I could not do any of this without your beautiful heart walking alongside mine.

Lifetimes traveled; we continue our march towards the light together. I wouldn't have it any other way. And for this I have felt to be one of the most blessed mothers in the world.

Thank you for your unwavering love and support. Thank you for your incredible wisdom revealed at exactly the perfect moment.

Thank you for sharing your beautiful, beautiful heart with me. Thank you for being here with your brilliant mind and blessed soul at this most incredible of times.
We're going to get there together.

There are more of you. And you know who you are. Thank you for your love, your support and friendship. Let's walk together and figure out the stuff that needs to be figured out. Hopefully with great anticipation in our hearts and some laughter along the way.

CONTENTS

Introduction

The world is not real. At least not in the way that you and I have been taught. It is an energetic world that resides within an energetic Universe. While this may not seem like something that you can easily accept, it is essential for you to understand in order for you to learn how to fully and limitlessly create in your life.

Quantum physics has shown us that the world and Universe at large is not made up of physical particles but actually space between energy. It is energy vibrating at different frequencies that can be directly correlated to the light and sound spectrum. And within those energetic frequencies, we as human beings vibrate within and are connected through the Heart's energetic field that it emits.

What does this mean to you at the everyday practical level of your life? It means that once you understand the fundamental energies that our Universe is made up of, operates within, and expresses through, then you become empowered as the divine and limitless creator that you truly are.

Each Chakra or energy center that resonates with every

aspect of our daily life is a channel in which we can tune into the varying frequencies of energetic vibration. Once you learn how to tune these different frequencies and bring them into a harmonic alignment at a conscious level with pure creative thought and feelings embraced, you can become the creative master of your life. And begin to live not only your destiny, but also a life filled with passion and purpose.

That's what this book is all about. To help you to understand that what you see, hear, smell and touch and feel is not all there is to this world. It's much, much more than that. And this is what everyone is waking up to at this incredible time on planet Earth.

We are all remembering. This book is here to help you remember. To jog those memories awake a little bit more. So that you and I can do what we came here to do. And that is to help wake others and help to change the world into one of peace, serenity and magnificent beauty. One of harmony and alignment. Of health and prosperity. One of enormous creative expression from each one of our hearts.

This is why we're all here now. And it is time to wake up and remember who we truly are, and what we are to do next. This is the Quiet Revolution of the Heart.

"If you want to find the secrets of the Universe, think in terms of energy, frequency and vibration."

Nikola Tesla

"You are an energetic being of great light, beauty and intelligence"

1

You Are Amazing

You are amazing. How do I know that you're amazing? I know because we are actually connected at a level that you can't see, smell, hear or touch, but you can definitely feel it when you understand that you are not a physical body in the way you've been taught to believe.

In fact, you are an energetic being of great light, beauty and intelligence. And this light, beauty and intelligence are the most real parts of who you truly are. You are just having a so-called human experience on this beautiful planet we call Earth.

Now this energetic body that you truly are vibrates at different frequencies that are then expressed through your human thoughts, feelings, words, actions and emotions. When you understand that your mind has the capacity to consciously create through focused intention, thoughts and feelings, you've just become the master of your life.

How can you become the master of your life? One of the best ways is to meditate each and every day. Because when you meditate you can bring your energy up in frequency and open your Heart to the wisdom of the Universe within.

And when you do this you can begin to remember the most important information you need to know now. And that is where you will begin to remember who you truly are, why you are here now and what you are to do next.

Why are these three remembrances so important to you now? Because Humanity needs you. We need your light, beauty and intelligence so we can find our way out of this mess we've somehow found ourselves in.

Humanity has reached its line in the sand and we've got two options starring us in the face right now. One is staying on the path of the fear-based paradigm designed to control us a collective resource. The other is the path of Love where limitless creative power, joy and Love reside.

Each of us will make our own choice as to what kind of world we want to create. I've already made mine and now I'm here to find my like-minded brothers and sisters who want to create a peaceful, harmonious life for them, their families and the future of all mankind. And last, but not by a long shot least, save our beautiful, beautiful planet in the process.

There is the very real potential that together we will destroy the very ecosystem that provides everything and more that we require to live, love and thrive. By the same token, that same very real potential is there to save Earth and Humanity. It's not as hard as it may seem, but it will require enough of us for a collective tipping point to be reached.

So now you can see how amazing each and every one of you truly are. And the incredible power you hold in your hearts and minds. And the difference that you can make as an individual because when we come together our collective minds and hearts can and will do amazing things, and literally make all the difference in the world.

So, this is how I already know how amazing you are. I already know that each one of you has the potential held inside of your heart to help save Earth and to directly contribute to collectively creating peace on Earth. That's possible. That's an amazing, beautiful and noble purpose that we've all come here to create together.

This time, this crazy, crazy time we're all living in is why we are here now. It's what each one of us came for. It's our clarion call to stand up and speak from our Hearts. It's our time to step into the very best version of who we came here to be.

We are living in the most exciting and exhilarating time in all of Humanity's history. We are finally able to remember who we truly are, why we are here now and what we are to do next.

This is amazing. You are amazing. And together we can do amazing things. We don't have to do the same thing except for one very, very, very important part. It's not hard or complicated. It doesn't require years of study or practice, a college degree or any technical skills. You don't need a WIFI connection, a computer or smart phone. You don't need money or even a bank account. You don't need a teacher, a guru or a priest. You simply need to open your Heart and love a little bit more each day.

When you envision Love radiating out and into the world from your Heart, you've just made a difference in the world. And it goes out into the energetic web that connects us all.

For those who can feel it – we will know that you've made your choice to love a little bit more each day. And as the days pass with you sending Love out from your Heart, you'll begin to see your life and the world from new eyes.

You'll begin to feel empowered. You'll begin to feel like who you truly are, and you'll begin to feel a gentleness come over you. Your words will be kinder. Your arms will wrap around others with more compassion, more understanding and more love. You'll smile more, laugh more and the desire to live with greater passion and purpose will rise out of your heart with great joy.

This time is what we've all been waiting for. It's why there are so many of us here. We came to do this thing called Love. We wanted to have a human experience where we could finally rise up and step into our own guru shoes.

Each one of us is an absolutely brilliant being filled with the limitless potential of the most powerful force in the Universe. And that power is Love. It's not the kind of power you use to manipulate and control through fear. Love is the power that creates Universes. Love is the power that creates life in all its forms.

This is what we've each been searching for and now you know why you are so amazing. And why you are here now. And what you are to do next. Love a little bit more each day. Say a kind word to someone as you pass by. Reach out and help someone who is struggling. We all know at least one person who is lost, or sad, or simply needs a hug and shoulder to lean on for a bit.

Share with them what you've learned here today. Lend a helping hand where you can. The world needs you now more than ever. I need you. The person next to you needs you. Together we will change the world one person at a time. Let's go there together, in Love, in Light and in the Beauty of Universal Intelligence that together we can create anything our Hearts and minds desire.

You are amazing.

"Within the macrocosm of the Universe lies the fundamental evolution of all life. Chaos stimulates crises to cause an effect for growth to take place."

2

In a Cosmic Nutshell

We are living in a time where the cosmic cycles of transformation have never been so transparent before. Within cycles of time there are periods where change and upheaval open doors to opportunities for growth otherwise not possible. This time is one of those cycles we all find ourselves in.

Within the macrocosm of the Universe lies the fundamental evolution of all life. Chaos stimulates crises to cause an effect for growth to take place.

There is a constant spiraling movement within all galaxies that reside within this Universe we currently exist within. Our solar system also moves within our Milky Way galaxy in the same way. Within the energetic gateway iconized by 2012 we are not only entering into the new 26,920-year cosmic cycle, but our Solar system has also entered into a new cosmic neighborhood in our galaxy. As such we are receiving new and different energies from the center of our galaxy. Similar to moving to a new country, the air is different, the light changes and our minds open to greater adventures and possibilities.

These new cosmic frequencies are received through our Sun and in turn the Sun is radiating them out to all of the planets within its system. This new energy carries a higher frequency of vibration that is stimulating our planet, all life and our bodies at every level of life.

This higher – or more refined energy is activating long dormant potential in our energetic system. Our nervous system is being stimulated and as a direct result our perceptions of time are shifting from one of focusing on the past to one of living in the creative potential of every moment.

Time as we knew it is all but gone. We are learning to live moment by moment. We are receiving these higher frequencies and our capacity to process new information is also expanding exponentially as a result. It is therefore easy to become over stimulated and overwhelmed as each of us makes the necessary adjustments along the way.

Within this synchronized cosmic cycle, you have a limitless dynamic, creative and chaotic collective participation by every human being on Earth.

One very important thing to do to balance the potential

resulting anxiety and over-stimulation is by integrating either a daily meditation or at minimum some time grounding yourself in Nature.

In addition to our nervous systems being upgraded, so too are our lives at every level. You may be experiencing any kind of life crisis, so be aware of the adjustments these energies are calling you to make.

A health crisis, big or small, is evidence that it is time to make changes you've resisted for far too long. Processing and releasing deep seated emotions and memories are the best place to start if you are experiencing a health crisis in particular at this time.

Even better is to take a long hard look before you experience something more severe. Emotional stagnation creates a backlog of energy eventually resulting in some sort of crises, regardless of where and how it shows up in your life.

Along with our perceptions evolving, so too is our awareness of the great imbalances in the world. What we as a collective thought was acceptable yesterday is no longer acceptable today. The glaring injustices that have been perpetrated at every level and sector of life are being called up for review and ultimately a dismantling from the inside out.

There is no culture among our collective Humanity who has not witnessed the atrocities of war, the subjugation of the female, spiritual beliefs or human suffering for expressing our individual rights of sovereignty.

Our innate divine heritage as human beings, of every sacred truth and especially the true nature of our creative potential have been systematically distorted and corrupted to distract and lead our hearts and minds as far away from Truth as the fear-based control paradigm could take us on an individual and collective level.

However, these new and higher frequencies, our new perceptions, our broadening awareness and our waking up are very quickly dropping the façade of the fear-based control paradigm curtain.

In a cosmic nutshell, this new energetic neighborhood we've moved into is the above and we are as a direct result creating the below, moment by moment with our new eyes to see the truths laid bare before us.

While facing some harsh realities of any wrongs done is never fun or necessarily easy, it is nevertheless a requirement before we can make the adjustments we are being called to make.

In all of life, there is first the desire for change, then the crisis to stimulate the actions needed to see the desired results. Living in a constant unchanging world is not possible. Change is the evolutionary constant in our world and stagnation of your unfulfilled desires and dreams is nothing more than succumbing to the fear-based resistance you try your very best to hold onto.

Embrace this time as a once in a lifetime opportunity to live your life like never before. Resurrect those long-hidden desires from within and let them out to play again. This is your time to jump in heart first and discover the exhilarating time we're all experiencing together. You can begin, big or small, just take the first step to dream a beautiful new dream from within, without and with the world around you. There is no better time than now.

"It is time for each one of us to reclaim our rightful place in the world as the Modern Day Goddesses we all are."

3

Modern Day Goddess

From a big picture view, this shift of the ages we're in is mostly about the re-emergence of the Divine Feminine Spirit. After millennia of taking a back seat, the full expression of the Divine Feminine is waking from her deep slumber along with humanity waking from their own.

This 'old guard' paradigm that has dominated our world and lives with its desire to control through power, greed and fear will continue to collapse as the compassion, love and creative strength of the Divine Feminine Spirit continues to nudge us awake a little more each day.

As the Divine Feminine energy continues to reestablish herself, through each and every one of us, (you too guys), we will all begin to experience a total freedom and release from a male-dominated world of bondage based on control through fear. For those of you who are women, you will want to utilize this re-emerging of your own Divine Feminine strength, will, and even sometimes, fierce determination, in every way in your own lives.

As women, mothers, sisters, daughters, grandmothers, and every other role that we women play in the world, it is our time to stand up and be heard. It is time for each one of us to reclaim our rightful place in the world as the Modern Day Goddesses we all are. It is what we are being called to do now.

From within each of our hearts the sparks of light within will begin to ignite other sparks of light within. Each one of us, in our own unique way, will begin to make a difference in the way that only we can do.

And in doing so, each one of us will directly contribute to creating a new world based on *limitless creation rather than controlled limitation.* This will ensure the health and safety of our Mother Earth, and for everyone who lives with her. It will be up to us to also ensure that the children of the world are safe and have enough of everything they need in order to grow and thrive.

On the other hand, if you continue to depend on the outer world through the established societal, governmental and religious structures to provide your perceived security, you will only find the fear that will continue to hold you in place as a slave to the empire that is crumbling. It is time now that we wake up to the truth that we are individually, as well as collectively, the creators of our world, and our lives in every way.

Your life is intended to be well lived through the many experiences of your expansive and unique ability for creative expression, not one of mere stagnant repetition and mediocrity. So, be brave, be courageous and do not fear change and the unknown. Live your life as the grand adventure it was intended to be.

Go out and make a difference in someone's life today. Take a chance and live the passion and joy that resides within your Heart. You'll discover that that is where true happiness and fulfillment reside.

As humanity continues to get out of bed, we will continue to see amazing new inventions and solutions to our biggest problems. This grand re-emergence of the Divine Feminine Spirit will be expressed in every form and facet through creative visionaries, whether in the form of fast-changing societal norms, innovative and sustainable energy resources, imaginative cultural styles of living, the creative arts, and new (actually ancient) healing modalities involving gems, light, sound and nature.

New innovative solutions are also quickly emerging to return not only our modern societies into harmonic expressions of cooperative living, but also in restoring a balanced and peaceful way of life for everyone. You will also see some of the greatest changes take place where individual creativity can be most easily expressed.

Expect to see the unexpected, as the Divine Feminine Spirit is the foundation for creative change and will be surprising us all in order to create the greater presence of her voice as a beacon for all to recognize and remember.

1.618

"On a collective level, our current cultural paradigm of life has been created by a thinking man's dream driven by fear, greed and competition."

4

A Game of Divine Proportion

There are more people on Earth than ever before. This population explosion is no mistake due to a lack of birth control or awareness, but because of the opportunity to experience the great equalization of the Divine Feminine and Divine Masculine Spirit coming back into balance again.

On a grand scale, we have collectively created this paradigm of living in a male-dominated world. Each one of us here today agreed to living lifetime after lifetime dominated by fear, power and greed, whether we played the role of the victim or the victimizer. Excited and curious to experience what it would be like to live under such circumstances of extreme imbalance and merciless control, our experiment has provided each and every one of us opportunities of learning otherwise impossible.

Of course, this required the blessing of our Mother – the Divine Feminine Spirit. To create such a game of divine proportion, we would need her cooperation to be subjugated, abused, raped and pillaged while living under the singular domination of the Divine Masculine out of balance with the natural order of life. Only the most loving Mother would agree to such a game so that we (her beloved children) could gain greater insight, wisdom and knowledge through these experiences.

And, now as our little experiment is just about over, with lifetimes of wisdom gained, both individually and collectively, we are still here and in even greater numbers than ever before at this pinnacle in time. Each of us has grown from surrendering ourselves to lifetimes of struggle, suffering, misery, and defeat.

We also lived lifetimes experiencing the power of willful control without compassion and greed at the expense of others. Whether living on either side of this coin, we all chose to experience the extreme separation from the innate compassion, love and grace of the Divine Feminine to keep it all in balance.

It's your individual choice if you want to start playing the new game of life with the Divine Feminine and Masculine Spirit restored to balance or stay in the old game of the Divine Masculine out of control. This is where each and every one of us will either cross the line in the sand or stay in our slumber and stay put under the thumb of control and domination.

As the Divine Feminine continues to re-emerge into her full and complete essence, and within each of our Hearts, she will also continue to exert and express her voice to the fullest in order to restore balance to the world, and in every way.

We are seeing it all around us. Women everywhere are feeling a renewed strength rise up from within. Many can no longer accept what they've put up with for years. They are crossing their own lines in the sand and taking control back over their lives. Voices are emerging and singing new songs of victory over victimization, solidarity over sexual abuse and definitely it's a 'my body' stance over any misogynist makings.

While returning the world to order and balance through her compassionate and loving heart, there are also those who are still slumbering and therefore unaware of what's really going on around them. Much like a deer caught in the oncoming headlights, many people today are similarly captivated by mainstream media's mesmerizing ability to keep them focused on the latest tragedy and near panic-evoking news.

While on one hand, the current state of the world, filled with more chaos, tragedy and fear than seen before, keeps many locked in fear, this is also clear evidence of the re-emerging Divine Feminine is bringing things back into balance.

The breaking down phase of the old guard is in full swing, and while it's frightening for many, all of the chaos and confusion actually serves a purpose in helping wake humanity from its deep slumber. There's nothing like great conflict and contrast to help those most resistant to change finally give in and surrender to making long overdue changes in their lives.

On a collective level, our current cultural paradigm of life has been created by a thinking man's dream driven by fear, greed and competition. Bringing it back to balance therefore will require compassion, justice and love.

Compassion to embrace the understanding that with all experience comes the opportunity to learn and grow.

Justice not in the man-made legal sense but a necessary adjustment to bring the damages done to light so that healing can take place. Healing not in the sense of forgetting, but with true forgiveness from the Heart can true growth only take place.

Love is the pure essence of all life and by its very virtue new life will spring forth from the ashes. What will be released will be replaced by a higher echelon of beauty in all its forms, including a higher expression of vibratory resonance within, without and with the world around you.

The Divine Feminine Spirit is the voice that whispers to you to follow your dreams and live your passions. She resides within your heart, and she is waking you now.

"The Universe is an intricately designed place with the limitless space to allow creative input, personal desires and spontaneous expansion to grow and evolve in."

5

Beauty

There is evidence all around us of this same divine proportion at the microcosmic levels of life as well. And nothing illustrates this more clearly than nature. Patterns of growth repeat themselves down to the microscopic level and beyond.

This pattern of design in the Universe can be seen in how leaves grow from a stem to the geometric proportions of the platonic solids, crystalline forms and sacred geometry. The Sunflower is one of my favorite examples of this divine proportion. Also, commonly referred to as the Golden Ratio or Phi it is represented by the number 1.618.

Even the Renaissance masters used this pattern of proportion in their art. They knew that if their painting was laid out to this proportional scale it would be more pleasing to the eye. And they were right.

DaVinci used it his Last Supper. Michelangelo used it in The Creation of Adam on the ceiling of the Sistine Chapel. The finger of God touches the finger of Adam precisely at the golden ratio point of the width and height of the area that contains them both. Raphael used golden ratios throughout his painting, The School of Athens. Botticelli also used it in his Birth of Venus. And the list goes on.

The Universe is an intricately designed place with the limitless space to allow creative input, personal desires and spontaneous expansion to grow and evolve in. Consider it a blank canvas that is constantly being painted. Layers of color added over the eons of time, your unique palette and brush add to the master canvas.

We may have been limited until now with the available brushes and skills at our disposal, however, that is all changing now. Much like painting with our left foot, and with only primary colors, we are about to use our hands with full palette and open heart.

As our perceptions of the world expand, our consciousness is waking up to new potential and creative abilities. Our apprenticeship is coming to a close and we are about to become the new Renaissance masters.

As we learn to paint our lives with masterly skill and a full palette, we will be exhibiting greater appreciation for beauty as well. Whether in the eye of the beholder or a finely tuned ear, beauty soothes the soul back to a centered and serene place.

The importance of Beauty in our lives is more important than ever today. More and more beauty is becoming under-appreciated and easily overlooked. Some would say the role of beauty in our lives is systematically being white-washed by the media's focus on producing anxiety and fear-inducing images and sounds. And the desired results are constantly being achieved with more and more negativity that is spewing out of every media channel and device at a dizzying pace.

So, it's an important reminder that beauty inspires. Beauty is an energy of positive charge that is like a food that sustains us at an elemental level of life. We are designed to feel good at an energetic level in order to be our best selves.

Feeling good opens doors and the gateway of Gratitude for all we have in our lives. When you feel good about your life you feel encouraged and inspired to do more. The blinders fall off and there is great potential in the moment.

When you gaze upon Beauty the appreciation for it shows you the limitless creative potential of life in a divinely creative Universe.

Go see Michelangelo's David and you will wonder with

amazement how he did it. Countless hours spent with chisel in hand to carve out this master of a seventeen-foot-tall man from a single piece of marble remains today as one of the world's greatest pieces of art ever created. Divine inspiration can be realized even under some of the most difficult of circumstances. It was a vision held in his heart and mind he held fast to until he achieved his masterful result.

It is these kinds of divine inspirations to create Beauty in all its forms that continue to inspire others to create their own masterpieces. The time it took for David to emerge into his final form has now stood as shining example of inspiration to countless others for over six hundred years.

The inspired vision, focused skill and relentless determination above and despite the physical demands, difficult work conditions and hardships tested Michelangelo beyond what most would succeed in overcoming today, much less dare to try.

However, the results at what he accomplished is a testament to the divinely-inspired purpose it continues to serve to this day.

So, if you once painted, or composed, or wrote poems of

love, start again. Or if you too are creating the masterpiece of your lifetime, persevere to the end no matter what challenges you face or obstacles you encounter. Creating something beautiful is always a worthwhile pursuit.

Art, music and all creative expressions serve this same purpose of divine inspiration. In our everyday lives, seeing a beautiful dress or piece of jewelry also acts as a catalyst for you to feel your best, or pretty, or beautiful in your own way.

These emotions elevate your vibration to a higher frequency. And in turn affect others as you go. Beauty at all levels of life definitely needs a reboot in today's world.

If it makes you feel good inside and inspired about life – do it. Then share it with others. You never know who you may inspire to create the next David.

"She has quietly waited and patiently watched while humanity has plundered and pillaged our way through countless battles, whether within our own hearts or out on the battlefields."

6

Every Day is Earth Day

The Divine Feminine Spirit resides in each and every one of us, regardless of our gender. She is also your Mother that you have long forgotten about, throughout eons of lifetimes, one after another. She has quietly waited and patiently watched while humanity has plundered and pillaged our way through countless battles, whether within our own hearts or out on the battlefields.

Our Divine Feminine Mother is the very real, alive and fully conscious being of beauty that we take for granted and casually call Earth. She too embodies the Divine Feminine Spirit that is re-emerging now.

And while this may sound obvious, without her, humanity cannot continue to exist. The absolute line in her dirt is quickly approaching and enough of us need to wake up and start making the necessary daily changes to collectively make a difference or before too long, our polluting the air, water, extracting and fracking her we will have cracked the Golden Goose who can sustain us no more.

Humanity must wake up and realize that every day is Earth day and take heed before it's really too late. There are countless little things we can do differently every day that collectively will make all the difference in the world – literally.

Recently I spent two weeks in Italy and at the end of our trip we had barely filled 2 small bags of garbage. I was astounded by the difference as compared to how much garbage we produce at home in California. This was a glaring example of how simply living more simply can have a big impact overall.

Eating fresh foods on a daily basis was the biggest difference. And all of the food we brought home – whether fresh-from-market fruits and veggies, cheese, milk or meat, they were all wrapped, packaged or placed in a recyclable material. I personally love re-using their 100% recyclable 'plastic' bags made from potato skins.

Like all Italians, we still bought bottled water as a necessity due to old pipes in ancient cities make for unhealthy drinking water. However, Italy has had an amazing system of recycling in place for many years. And they are constantly making improvements.

While the larger recycling dumpsters still sit on many streets, Florence has installed bins that you tap a lever with your foot to open it and then simply drop your bottles and cans in one, your paper and cardboard in another, and even your organic waste in yet another. The separated garbage is then collected along the city streets.

In many towns, there are also conveniently located battery bins along the streets making recycling your used batteries as convenient as it can get.

I live in a large apartment complex in Los Angeles, with over six hundred units, and there is no recycling system here. The best they've managed is to have two relatively small dumpsters in the parking garages for cardboard boxes. Otherwise I have to drive to a can and plastic recycling location, and more often than not, wait in line to recycle my plastic and cans. There is no effectively organized recycling system in this sprawling city of over 4 million people.

One of the most needed recycling systems on a global scale is that of electronic waste. If many people are buying the latest smart phone every year, or updating to the latest ipad or laptop, where are all of the old ones going?

Some e-waste recyclers are shipping boatloads of old electronics to third-world nations, and they are simply piling them up in waste-yards. This exposes the environment and the local people working to recover valuable materials such as copper and gold to over 1,000 harmful substances. Some of the worst e-waste hazards are mercury, lead, cadmium, barium, hydrocarbons, flame retardants and lithium.

Unfortunately, there are more than 18 million children and adolescents working with e-waste recycling because their small hands are more dexterous than adults. In addition, many pregnant women are also involved in working with e-waste, leaving them as well as their unborn child to the dangerous effects of the harmful materials.

The short list of the potential negative health effects of these toxins include brain, heart, liver, kidney, DNA and skeletal damage. Still-birth, premature births as well as lung function and respiratory issues.

The good news is that there are some great new e-waste recyclers starting to address this issue now, so be on look and make sure you recycle your e-waste responsibly.

This is one more example that has the potential for far reaching effects. And opportunity. Anyone could devise a system of efficient e-waste and household waste recycling within their own community. Or simply duplicate what the

Italians are doing here. New businesses and increased prosperity are waiting around the next corner for those open to see it.

"All of the little choices we make add up to an overall energetic frequency that we individually tune into."

7

Choice Points

Each one of us is living at a frequency level created by everyday choices that we make, one by one, day by day. All of the little choices we make add up to an overall energetic frequency that we individually tune into.

Choosing to eat fast food rather than a healthy salad is a choice point that will drop your energy to a lower frequency by the no-energy food you're eating rather the high-energy healthy salad you were going to eat when you got home.

Or choosing to watch a crime drama on TV versus a comedy is another small choice but has exponentially larger energetic results. Watching a fear or suspense-provoking drama drops you into a low frequency state and into the fight or flight reactive mind quickly. It's the equivalent to stepping out of your cognitive mind and seeing only two options before you. When your energy drops to the fear frequency you also become extremely vulnerable to control agendas that want to hold you in place like a deer caught in headlights.

For eons this is where Humanity as a collective has been held and systematically programmed to believe in a paradigm of fear, competition and control. Many of today's cultural beliefs, religious dogma and governmental laws have been purposely designed to restrain, restrict and limit the individual's full expression of their innate and creative potential.

Here is where you can begin to separate the wheat from the chaff. You can take your discernment back by stepping out of the fear when you no longer choose to expose yourself to it. Simply take the good parts and leave the rest. There is wisdom and value in all of what Humanity has created together.

The point is to see things for the way they've evolved and not turn a blind eye or follow the crowd. Ask the questions that need to be asked at every level of life. Be honest with yourself so that the new choices you make begin to lift you up and into a higher state of frequency.

When you educate yourself on how to make new choices, you will be elevating your frequency and taking Humanity with you. When your collective choices add up and lift you out of resonating at the level of frustration or hopelessness or a general dissatisfaction with your life, your new frequency will also help to elevate others as well.

It's not an overwhelming goal to achieve your destiny when you understand that your life is made up of all the little decisions you make along the way.

In any moment you can choose to be happy. In any moment you can recall a memory and feel sad or angry all over again. That argument you had that led to a break up was made up of choices you made in each moment.

You had the option to not feel hurt by what he said. Hurt feelings are a choice you make to feel hurt. If someone says something to you that you then decide was mean or hurtful, that is your choice in the moment – and sometimes long after - to feel that way.

Another person cannot make you feel any one way or another. It's just their opinion in that moment. If you are confident and know who you are from the inside, that awareness will support you to step out of the subjective self in moments where you can choose to not be hurt.

This will be easier for some people and harder for others. It may be that you chose to experience certain choice points in this lifetime in order to grow.

However, in the big picture of Humanity's current process of evolving into a higher frequency as a collective species, one major theme that is playing out on a global scale is getting off the victim train and standing in our individual responsibility of the choice points that add up to our lives.

When you remove the role of victim from your frequency scale, you've just made the choice to liberate yourself from the playing the role of slave to your emotions, your lack of power, your lack of success, your lack of vitality or health or whatever you have been "powerless" to create in your life thus far.

When you choose to be one hundred percent responsible for your life, you empower yourself to step into becoming the limitless creator you are destined to be.

It is a choice. And you are free to choose it in any moment. Your mind belongs to you, and when you take your attention off the many media distractions designed to keep you mesmerized and under the thumb of the old fear-based control paradigm, you are reclaiming your innate power to create. No one can take your mind without your consent and cooperation.

If you are unhappy in your life or simply dissatisfied with something you want to change or improve, start by making new choices. Begin by choosing what you want your life to look like. Then break it down to the little decisions you'll need to make in order to elevate yourself to that higher frequency. You won't see results on the outside until you make the necessary adjustments on the inside.

This may require some work you'll need to do. Make the time and space to do the work and before long you'll be seeing positive results in your life.

While there's no denying we're living in a time of heightened chaos and confusion, we are also experiencing a time of great opportunity for Humanity to pull itself together and turn things around.

"Remember that as a conscious being you have the amazing capacity to stop the emotional chaos, get quiet and go within your Heart's innate wisdom to the solutions."

8

Phoenix Rising

Conscious evolution is taking place before our very eyes on the macrosm/microcosm levels. Along with Mother Earth our vibratory essences are being elevated to new heights, with the debris of our past falling away as quickly as we can let it go.

Big or small, everyone at some level of life is experience a crisis, calamity or challenge. It's no coincidence that at an individual level the cosmic winds of change are affecting us all. It's time to clear the cobwebs of the past and allow new light to stream into our hearts.

When you're facing a challenge or crisis in your life there are two possibilities as to the cause.

1. You have self-sabotaged yourself into the situation through fear and worry, or –
2. You consciously planned this event in your life

lesson plan as a catalyst to get your attention to make some necessary changes in your life.

You as the creator can choose how your life runs. As in any moment facing raging seas of emotions you can always find the calm center and solutions to every life storm. Always.

Remember that as a conscious being you have the amazing capacity to stop the emotional chaos, get quiet and go within your Heart's innate wisdom to the solutions.

It takes a little discipline and awareness to recognize the emotional turmoil is actually being created by you, the experiencer. You can choose in any given moment to stop the reactionary and judgmental merry-go-round and get off and get your equilibrium back.

When you are willing to take responsibility for your own thoughts, actions and words you will be stepping into the magnificence of who you truly are. As this is one of the most empowering and self-liberating moments a person can have. Now you will begin to recognize the true creative power you hold within.

The next step will be to practice conscious awareness and responsibility for every thought, action and word you express. Self-awareness is the key to begin living the life you designed, desire and are destined to live to your greatest potential.

In order for all healing and transformation to take place the shadows must be revealed. Much like the phoenix rising from the ashes of the fires, what no longer serves each one of us must undergo a process of healing. This healing goes through its own process involving three steps to transformation:

Step 1: Recognition. Conscious recognition of the missteps or perceived mistakes we feel we have made in our lives. Including the intentional wrongs done to others, however justified in our minds and hearts. All of the perceived hurts, anger, resentments and blame that we have projected onto to others as well as what we have held within for way too long.

Step 2: Responsibility. Conscious responsibility for the decisions and choices we made that contributed to or created all of the above. Taking responsibility for your part in relationships that have failed or fallen apart is the key to healing all past wounds. It is time now to remember how to heal and grow beyond our wounding. It's why we are here now.

Step 3: Release. Consciously letting all of the emotional baggage go. Once you've worked through Step 2 it is possible to release the memories and energetic debris you've been holding onto for way too long. Emotional memories are actually negative energy pockets and can easily get stuck at the cellular level. If the emotions are powerful enough, such as deep-seated anger or resentments, they can eventually manifest as chronic or even life-threatening disease.

All disease starts at an emotional level. In fact, the origin of the word disease is; dis-ease. Forgiveness is the key to releasing all negative memories. Forgive yourself as well as the other parties involved. It's a process and will require time, effort and energy. It will be worth it.

Then feel the gratitude baby. No life is lived well without feeling grateful for all that you do have. Gratitude will open new doors faster than anything. It must be heartfelt and with the acceptance that you don't always know what's in your own highest good. Leave that up to your Higher Self and allow the Universe to do what it does best by bringing you the synchronistic connections and perfect timing into play.

"The reality of our reality is that the only real constant is change."

9

Change is the Only Constant

When things don't look the way we want or expected, that's when it's time to stop and review what's really going on inside.

This is when you'll want to ask yourself some tough questions. It's not always easy to be totally honest with ourselves. It is however easy to make excuses or blame others for where we end up at certain points in our lives.

It is also very easy to get complacent, to ignore the signs or to go along with the status quo or maybe even give up. It's not easy to look in the mirror and admit the compromises you've made along the way or looking the other way when you needed to stand up, speak up or simply walk away.

Life can be full of challenges, but these are all opportunities to grow and expand your awareness, your understanding, your compassion, and your ability to give and receive.

If you wipe away the tears of frustration, hurt, pain and anger you will find the opportunity in every experience to discover something about yourself that needs adjusting from within.

When we judge others for their misdeeds or frustrating behavior, demeanor or communication style, something within is calling your attention to it. If your buttons are getting pushed, they are like your alarm clock within to wake up to changes you need to make within yourself.

Self-reflection is hard when you've learned that judgment and blame are the answer to your problems. It's always about the other person who has done something 'to you'. The truth is that it's really all about you.

You attract people into your life for lessons that you chose to learn. We live in a Universe that operates through a finely tuned symphony of energy, vibration and frequency. So, if your current sound of music is out of tune, discordant or keeps playing the same 'ol chorus over and over again, it's time to tune yourself up. Once you learn how to maintain your harmonies from within, you'll get the hang of auto-tune and begin moving up the harmony scale.

Life will not always be perfect on the outside. You've got lessons to learn and that's why you are here now. However, you can definitely ease the way with fewer bumps in the road when you become willing to do the work and ask yourself the tough questions.

Taking responsibility for what's going on the inside of you is the first step. That's when you step out of the judgement and blame game and choose to become the victor in your life rather than the victim.

You'll feel a great sense of renewal from within when you realize this and truly engage yourself in being honest about where you are and what needs to change to get you where you want to be.

Life viewed with a new perspective opens you up and your life becomes the grand adventure it is intended to be. And maybe with a little drama, excitement and cliff hanging moments along the way, but that's really what we came for.

Those cliff hangers of your life act as catalysts for change. Sometimes we need them in order to wake up and make some adjustments. Change is frightening to many. It's uncomfortable for most. And yet there are others who thrive on change and new adventures.

The reality of our reality is that the only real constant is change. We live in a dynamic world that is constantly on the move. When you combine the frequencies of seven billion plus unique symphonies into one collective composition, you'll end up with a lot of disharmony and noise.

Imagine what we could sound like if we harmonized our hearts with the Universal Frequency of Love. Resistance would give way to a collective symphony of acceptance, compassion, beauty and love.

Hate would dissolve into love. Judgement would disappear into compassion. Resistance into acceptance. Beauty would ensue at every level of life and humanity would move up the frequency scale and embrace the evolutionary leap that lay before us now.

The everyday petty frustrations, judgments and constant resisting the outer chaos all starts within and coalesces into the big picture of the 'out there' and 'what currently is'.

The more you get this, the sooner your life and the world will begin to express a more harmonic song of love and compassion. We're here together and are now being called on to embrace each other's journeys with acceptance, respect and compassion.

No one can know why someone else is living the way they do. It's not your job to judge. Just begin each day to let go of paying so much attention to the chaos that currently surrounds you and start to create the centered calm from the inside out. That will work wonders in your life and in the world, one person at a time.

"Secrets held and hidden for too long are being revealed in order to be healed."

10

A New Renaissance

If some area of your life is falling apart, be encouraged and embrace the breaking down phase of transformation. As without moving through clearing out the cobwebs from the corners of your life, true breakthroughs for creating lasting improvements will not happen.

Along with the crumbling of worn-out facades is the transparency that is being called for more and more. Calling a spade, a spade is not always pretty or pleasant but a necessary shift from blinders on to blind truths.

Secrets held and hidden for too long are being revealed in order to be healed. There is no honesty in pretending any longer. Whether you are ready to jump in or hesitantly dip your toes into the water, the opportunity is knocking on the door to your Heart to begin living love as a lifestyle.

What does that mean, living love as a lifestyle? It means that you are no longer willing to hide in the shadows of long held anger or resentments. It means you are willing to be open, honest and responsible for every word you speak and everything that you do.

It means there are no hidden agendas, no desires to compete or win. No goals to conquer or gates to close. It means compassion rules the day and the passion for your life is palpable from the inside out.

It means that you now walk your yellow brick road and follow your heart to the Emerald City of your Hearts true wisdom. It means that fear no longer holds you back from hearing the whispers of your Heart's true desires.

It means there is a new Renaissance taking place within each one of us. It means the desires and dreams you've repressed are stronger and can no longer be ignored or pushed aside.

We are here now to participate in Humanity's evolutionary process. Together. The struggle to maintain some kind of equilibrium is real for many now. If you are ahead of the evolutionary curve, reach out and share your experiences, your knowledge and wisdom to help guide others through their transformational process.

We are here to support each other, to love each other and to act as beacons of inspiration whenever possible. There is no going it alone. We are not alone. Ever. If isolation is what you're currently experiencing, then get out and get help.

Once you open up to the limitless opportunities available to us all, the Universe will respond with the synchronicities to lift you up and out of isolation and connect you to the next step.

This new renaissance requires each one of us to do our part and contribute our experiences, our knowledge and wisdom with others. It's what we came here to do. Your experiences have prepared you for this time. As a collective you, your unique perspective is of value to the collective whole. It also enables you to relate to others who are going through similar experiences.

That makes you an expert on how to move through a crisis and learn from it. This is a valuable contribution each one of us can make while helping others heal their way through to the light within again.

Don't underestimate the value of life's toughest

tribulations. They all hold wisdom within and if you have succeeded in grasping this successfully, you have wisdom gained that you need to share now.

Embracing change is the comfort required to truly rise to the challenges of evolutionary transformation. Entering the frictionless space of your heart places you in a resistance-free state where all possibilities reside.

This is the space you want to be in. It is waiting for you to simply release the grip on all anger, judgment, resentments and hurts held within for way too long.

It's the slip stream of your life where no paddle is required. Enter this quiet space and the calm and serenity will empower you to step out of the fear paradigm and into the quiet revolution of your Heart.

And when you do, you will not look back but to the future of a new renaissance from within, without and with the world around you.

"As healing takes place at the individual level, the collective will adjust along the way, restoring balance in both men and women".

11

Balance is the Key

This time is not about Feminism or creating a Feminist movement. This is not about women rallying against men. Suddenly judging another for trespasses twenty or thirty years past is not the kind of leveling the playing field the Divine Feminine Spirit requires in order to restore balance. While pointing out the obvious errors of captains of industry, government and religious structures will have an overall effect; there is a desired balance point in the healing process as well.

So, there will need to be consideration and a higher expression of the damages done within our collective sights set in restoring balance through compassion. Remember that we all come into our lives to play a role, big or small, and to learn the lessons we chose to learn. We need to be the examples of leading the collective way back to balance without sinking into the lower frequencies of retaliating with venomous words and accusations.

The eons of control and abuse by men at all levels of life are no secret to anyone, so the countless favors for play, sexual intimidation all the way through the most horrific acts against the female species do not now need to be the protest slogan for the Divine Feminine Spirit.

As healing takes place at the individual level, the collective will adjust along the way, restoring balance in both men and women. Adjustments will occur within each one of us, creating a higher expression of recognition, respect and compassion for all, as we don't want to now create a new imbalance by being vindictive and retaliatory in the process.

Without question, it is a fine line to be walked, and however you feel about the wrongs done by men through the ages; there are also countless good and decent men as well. Let's be cautious not to let the bad apples spoil the entire barrel.

Women everywhere are feeling the renewed sovereignty and empowerment from within and will no longer compromise themselves or their bodies to anyone. This is the level of awareness we as women and men need to now express and exemplify for each other.

So be the shining example of the Divine Feminine and lead the way back to balance that you came here to be. Be the change you want to see in the world from within, without and with the world around you.

Imagine the world you want to live in, a world that expresses Nature's beauty and bounty with effortless creative expression. A world where people everywhere are the embodiment of the Divine expression each came here to be.

It is a reality a breath away from being before you as the potential always lay within the desire, the vision and passion to bring it forth into expression.

Once you begin to focus your attention on what you do want, rather than all that is wrong with the world will you begin to truly create the world in which you desire to live in.

This is as simple as it sounds, however many still sit glued to their TVs believing in a world created by those whose sole desire is to keep you captivated by the fear-based paradigm of control.

Take back your mind and heart and allow your innate wisdom to emerge from within. Your mind is designed for your imagination to paint the pictures you want to see.

Your heart is the gateway to all of the wisdom of the Universe, designed for each one of us to enter and gaze upon the limitless Love the Universe holds within. Untapped potential lies within each one of us to access, explore and begin creating a new life and world for all.

Imagine a world of unspoken beauty, compassion and love. A world filled with cooperation, abundance and health for all rather than a few. A world where your unique expression of unfettered creativity will create the next millennium of unbridled freedom to express who you truly are.

These are but a few of the concepts open to each one of us now. Step through the doorway of your Heart and enter into the new paradigm of life on Earth. Your ability to open your mind and Heart are the only perceived limitations before you.

Align yourself with Love, Compassion and Beauty in every waking moment and watch your world shift from one of limitation to one of great Abundance. This is not a promise but pure potential and each one of us can choose it in any given moment. The idea that some are not worthy is a distortion based on a scarcity-based paradigm designed to keep you out of touch with your true potential.

Reach for the stars and stay open to all possibilities. They are finally within your reach. Practice your imaginings of a beautiful world filled with all good things, not only for yourself, but for all.

In the effort to imagine a perfect world will the tides begin to turn, and new ideas will emerge and begin to replace an old and outworn paradigm.

Step into who you truly are and discover the potential within. And as you do, more will be revealed from within. It is the time for Humanity to begin its transformation into a cooperative and contributing people of Love, Harmony and limitless creative expression.

"Because we are all intimately connected through the energetic connectedness of our Hearts and the Universe, we as individuals and as a collective species have a *direct and causal impact* on the 'real' world around us."

12

The Quiet Revolution of the Heart

As the pendulum continues to swing back to center, and as our own awakening process picks up speed, you will be seeing more and more evidence of waking hearts all around you and in every sector of life.

As we wake up, our increasingly integrated Heart-centered selves will recognize that things are not as they should be, and certainly life can in no way continue without some significant adjustments and recalibrations along the way.

In a very real sense, it is actually the collective consciousness of Humanity as it awakens that is causing the tremendous chaos that is taking place as you read this. Because we are all intimately connected through the energetic connectedness of our Hearts and the Universe, we as individuals and as a collective species have a *direct and causal impact* on the 'real' world around us.

It appears that this would be a question of which comes first, the chicken or the egg? However, when you conceive of an idea, or question the validity of a system, process, institution, or any other person, place or thing, that very question or idea creates a wave of energy that acts as a trigger in the connective web of energy in which each one of us lives, expresses and exists within. This is exactly how each one of us can, and actually does make a real difference in the world.

With the looming big issues facing us in our daily lives and global community, at every level of life, most people feel insignificant and incapable of affecting real change as a single person. However, when you fully understand the energetic system of our life, our environment, our world and even the Universe, the light goes on and you finally 'get it'.

Our biggest challenges today can easily be solved by simply getting it. For when you open your mind, heart and soul to the limitless possibilities of the creative Universe in which we exist, the solutions will naturally emerge through innovation and new thought inventions. In addition, many of the daily choices we make would become glaringly obvious in the way they *directly contribute* to the biggest issues facing us now, both in our personal lives as well as how they impact our world on a grand scale.

One of the most important shifts in awareness you can consciously choose to make, is to simply take your focus off of the negative news, chaos and all of the things that you think, judge or believe to be 'bad' in the world. Then begin to consistently focus your attention on what is beautiful and joyful in your own life, and in the world.

When you stop putting your attention, which is energy, on all of the bad news in the world, you are making a real and effective change by withdrawing *your energy* from *contributing* to those events and circumstances. You are making the conscious decision to no longer support with your life force the very things you do not want to see in the world any longer.

When enough people make this same simple shift in focus, the 'bad' things can in no way continue to exist. One by one, our collective energy will no longer create, nor support the very things we don't want in our world and lives.

Get very clear with your understanding of this concept, as it is absolutely critical to your creative success in your life.

When your focus, attention and energy are expressed as *resistance* against any perceived wrong, you are actually contributing your life force energy to the very thing you don't want.

The only energetic response the Universe can respond to resistance energy is; more reasons for you to express your judgment, anger and resistance. That is the energetic blueprint you are sending out, often with a lot of emotional energy behind it. You are telling the Universe to keep sending you the same perceived wrongs for you to react to from an emotionally charged and reactionary state. It's a simple case of like attracts like.

One paradigm of life ruled by a system of domination and control will not simply and suddenly agree and say, okay, you guys are right, and we are wrong. It just will not happen that way. As Einstein said, "You cannot solve the problem with the same mind that created it."

By the same token, when you shift your focused attention on all of the beauty of the world, the amazing creativity and abundance that life truly offers, then you will be creating real change for the better not only in your own life, but also for the world at large.

This is the true power waiting to be unveiled. This is the Quiet Revolution of the Heart. Where there are no guns required, no protests needed, no taking to the streets, and certainly no violent revolutions that will somehow affect positive change. You simply cannot change a system of domination and control, with the very same approach of expressing your forceful desires against it.

To create a new paradigm of life on Earth, will by necessity require a new way of thinking. And, as the current male dominated world is expressed through the Divine Masculine Spirit, then the obvious shift would be to begin to 'think' more with our Hearts, and not the logical mind so much.

Allowing yourself to follow your Heart, rather than allowing your logical mind to take the lead, is the real shift in consciousness that we're all being asked to make now. And, following your Heart is where all the magic starts and real fun begins to take place.

When you get the mind out of the driver's seat and allow your Heart to take the wheel, you will not only be happier, but you will jump into the stream of limitless abundance, creativity and joy. This is when all the lights go on, and the difference in how you feel at every level becomes palpable in every way. Your innate creativity resides at a very real energetic level and is your direct conduit to all of the wisdom and infinite knowledge of the Universe. It is also when you really get 'turned on' as the divine and limitless creator that you truly are.

Once you recognize, reclaim and begin to reinvent the world, from the inside out through expressing our newly reclaimed Divine Feminine Spirit, you will by nature inspire others to do the same. And as we transform ourselves, remember that the Quiet Revolution of the Heart begins.

"Anything less than Love is a diminished expression toward the shadow spectrum of the lower frequency scale."

13

Love Makes the World Go 'Round

Love is the elixir of all life. It is the creative energy of the Universe each one of us holds within our Hearts. Anything less than Love is a diminished expression toward the shadow spectrum of the lower frequency scale. Therefore, coming back to center and accessing the wisdom of Love held within is the solution to every life challenge you face now. Regardless of what kind of crisis you are facing today, the answers lay within.

From minor confusion to major life crisis, your Heart can lead you back to center, clarity and a renewed state of being. Personal choice is always available in every moment. If you have planned a crisis to learn a life lesson, then you may feel that your options are closed.

However, you choose to deal with any challenge in life, understanding that you can always choose to move through them with grace and Love is an option open to everyone.

Sinking into the lower frequency emotions of self-pity, anger, frustration or hopelessness is not the answer. These lower emotions feel bad to you as an indicator to get back to center and to feel and express the Love you hold within.

Easier said than done you may say, however in all things the more practice you make the easier it gets. And no practice is better spent now than going within and connecting to the Universal frequency of Love in your Heart.

You can start by simply taking five minutes each day to get quiet and feel gratitude for all you have in your life. Feeling grateful will bring you into your Heart faster than anything else you can do. Then just remain quiet, continue feeling the gratitude and then listen closely for the whispers of guidance from within. The more you do this the greater clarity you will gain to see your way out of your challenge.

Love is the greatest guidance you can seek. Love dispels all disharmony, friction and resistance energy in every kind of situation. Out of every storm Love will lead you to your true Hearts desires and calm, centered seas.

Feel Love for the beautiful Earth you call home. Express that Love to her. Envision your arms wrapping around her with Love and gratitude.

Love is the greatest power in the Universe, yet we have been systematically led away from it at every level of life. Societal structures have been emphasized as the more important pursuits in life. And those distractions have never been more glaringly obvious than now.

From the combative and unbelievably divisionary politics of today's world to the constant focus on celebrity news, fashion distraction and material status, it's a wonder anyone can think straight anymore.

These media machinations have been purposely designed to divide and conquer the masses and keep us mesmerized by the non-stop media frenzy of feeling less-than along with the frenetically-paced fear provoking news. Take your mind back by taking your attention and focus off these media-induced lower frequency distractions.

Outside of something funny, although much of today's humor is about the craziness of the current state of the world, ask yourself when was the last time you felt good inside after watching TV? It serves no one other than the control paradigm's agenda. Taking your time, energy and focus off the media is an important step you can take now to regain your focus and discernment.

Unless you want to stay in the lower frequencies of conflict, judgment, resistance, shock and disgust, stop watching all mainstream news media. All of the evidence that our politicians to the President serve a different master than the people has been very clearly presented. You have all the proof you need to understand things need to change. So, does a continuous sense of outrage and combative diatribe amongst us affect any real change?

Is arguing with "the other side" going to change their views and convictions? And if you were able to eventually sway someone into agreement would that make a difference overall?

It's not about not speaking up or expressing your views on the 'what is'. It's about channeling your energy and focus in a positive way so that real change can take place. Find your like-minded friends and discuss ideas and solutions that you would like to see happen in the world. That is how you can make a difference. Create a new system, a new process, a new format, a new way of anything that is in the highest and best interest of the all rather than the few.

This is how each one of us can take back our true power and voice. This is how we regain our balance and begin to restore sanity in the world. When you take your focus off all that is "wrong" with the world, or your life, you will be withdrawing your energy from actually perpetuating those very things you are judging to be bad or wrong.

Once enough of us are no longer willing to engage in these societal conflicts, and simply focus on the solutions, the old game of divide and conquer can no longer continue. This works at every level of life. If someone wants to argue with you yet you choose to walk away, no argument can ensue.

The same is true at the collective level. When there are enough of us no longer willing to play in their paradigm of controlled fear it can no longer exist. However, a tipping point must be reached with enough people shifting their focus and energy from fear to Love. It does not require us all, but a relatively small percentage to reach this 'hundredth monkey effect' to be reached in order to shift the paradigms.

It's important for you to understand that you are critical to making a difference in the world now. You could be that 'hundredth monkey' and tip the scales toward the new Love paradigm. So, please don't underestimate the importance of your role and purpose in these times.

Everyone makes a difference and there is no greater sense of urgency than now to make your own choice in which world you want to collectively create. Choosing to stay in a world of divisive fear-based propaganda only means that at some level you are not ready to embrace Love and move up the frequency scale of learning.

Everyone is on their journey and will choose which way they want to go at the perfect moment for them. Honor that choice and respect everyone's personal journey. Once you accept this you will see judgment fall away more in your own life.

"If you want to live your life full of creative wonder, loving relationships, optimum health, financial abundance, and living with passion and purpose, you'll want to keep your Chakras open and humming in harmonic alignment."

14

Your Energetic Immune System

We are living in an energetic Universe that is constantly on the move. And, your Chakras carry the energetic blueprints for every area of your life within that energetic Universe. In order to create your life, the way you want it to be, you must follow the fundamental steps of creating it first at the energetic level. This requires you to move through each step in the Universal Law of Creation.

If you want to live your life full of creative wonder, loving relationships, optimum health, financial abundance, success and living with passion and purpose, you'll want to keep your Chakras open and humming in harmonic alignment.

If you understand that everything is made up of the same energy, and your body is also part of this energy, then it becomes obvious to see the innate connection you have with everyone and everything in the world. Therefore, you do make an impact, and everything that you do and say also impacts this grand field of energy like a sound wave goes out to be heard, or a ripple in the water moves out into the sea.

While we have been taught that our physical bodies are made up of matter, quantum physics shows us that there is no such thing as physical matter, but only a grand field of energetic potentiality. This field of 'new physics' also shows us that when we place our attention upon the smallest observable particles, the simple act of our observation actually affects these tiniest of energetic particles.

It works the same way with everything that we do, think, say and believe, as it all goes out and affects the world in ways unseen, yet is nevertheless there.

Your day to day life, moment by moment is actually created by the vibrational frequencies you express within the perceived third dimensional reality we are currently experiencing.

Your life, your pets, your family and friends and everything you see, feel, smell and touch are perceptions based on an energetic resonance. Your thoughts, feeling, emotions, desires and dreams are what either propel or magnetize your perceptions into the current reality you are experiencing.

When you fully understand how your energy flows within the framework of the Universe at large, you will begin to see the greater game we are all playing in. Once you grasp the concept you will free yourself from the equally limiting perceptions of stagnation and ill health. Once you perceive the grand scale of the energetic resiliency you possess, your creative outlets for expression will multiply exponentially.

However you choose to utilize this information is up to you. You can question and explore limitless possibilities, or you can choose to stay in the status-quo comfort of nonchalance or blind ignorance. Equally important is the knowledge that you are free to choose in any given moment to create and manifest your next adventure and experience.

While many continue to live by default and feel powerless in their lives, I suggest you make a game of it and test these concepts for yourself. At the very least, you may be surprised at what you discover. For those who are curious and open-minded enough to try, take a cautionary tale and start by carefully choosing what it is you want to create.

Simply wanting to create millions of dollars is not utilizing your creative mastery to its utmost potential. Better to start small and with something that will not cause a tidal wave of subsequent dominoes falling in a direction unintended.

Now that you know that everything in the world is made up of energy, it is also important to better understand how that energy is organized. How do we as individuals interact with this field of energy, and how are we also affected by it?

We are actually experiencing our daily lives through a multidimensional energetic system that allows us to not only experience and express ourselves in a multitude of ways, but we are also creating each minute of our lives through our reacting, interacting, interpreting, expressing, perceiving, and of course, consciously creating our daily lives, moment by moment in a vast sea of collective multidimensional experiences.

Let's break it down into each aspect of how we operate as human beings within this multidimensional energetic system we simply call life on Earth. Let's also look at the fundamentals of how we experience our lives through our human selves. You have several levels to what I call your Energetic Immune System that makes up the 'you' that you innately are.

The Physical Body

You already know that you have a brain that operates much like a computer in order for the body to function properly and maintain optimum health and longevity. This is the 'control center' for both the thinking and auto-pilot-basic body functions, along with the newly discovered heart-brain intelligence; we function as our physical selves as we move through our daily lives.

Your physicality is currently experienced and expressed through the perceived paradigm of third-dimensional reality. Your physical body relates and experiences to the outer world through the Heart's Intelligence and the mundane five senses: touch, sight, sound, taste and smell at the Root Chakra, Sacral and Solar Plexus energy centers.

The Emotional Body

Within the Emotional Body reside your emotions, thoughts, desires, beliefs, and memories, which represent the other aspects of your perception of how you experience your everyday life and is most commonly experienced through the 'gut level' or Solar Plexus Chakra energy center.

Your everyday emotions act as a guide for you to experience what feels good or bad and everything in between. It allows you to experience the full spectrum of emotions through life in its many facets and expresses, operates and connects to others through your Solar Plexus.

Your Emotional body also connects you to others through shared experiences as mirrors and teachers for greater compassion, love, acceptance, allowing, and joy to enter into your life through the Heart and Higher Heart Chakras.

You have probably heard the saying that like attracts like. That's all well and good at a thought-based level, however as human beings, our lives are not based on thinking alone. In fact, when it comes to living in an energetic Universe, where everything is made up of the same energy, feelings are far more important and powerful on an energetic level than thoughts are.

Your feelings and how you express your emotions are the tour de force to consciously creating and magnetizing the experiences you truly want to bring into your life. Your emotions and how you experience them are part of the Universe's energetic elixir that is required in any recipe for delight or disaster in your life. And the stronger the emotion, the stronger the wave of energetic force that goes out into the Universes mixing bowl of new recipes.

You can begin to create more positive emotions by practicing the following:

- ☐ Forethought
- ☐ Emotional resilience
- ☐ Heightened perception
- ☐ Personal responsibility
- ☐ Conscious awareness

The Heart Center

Your Heart, both in its physical function and as the balance point within the body's Energetic Immune System connects to all life in the Universe through its holographic torus field. Your heart holds within it the divine aspect of who you truly are, why you are here now and what you are to do next. Your heart is the gateway to your greatest joy, your greatest achievements and all of the wisdom of the Universe. Living from the heart is *the key* to living a life full of peace, harmony and joy, *despite* the chaos that surrounds you.

The Heart's Higher Emotional Body

The frequency of Universal Love can be accessed through the Higher Heart center, through which the higher emotions can be experienced and expressed. When it is open, and you are in energetic alignment with it, you can access and experience the higher emotions of joy, bliss and ecstasy. These higher emotions are easily experienced through practicing gratitude for everyone and everything in your life.

Appreciating the great beauty of Nature, along with the higher forms of creativity through art, music and the written word can also create energetic gateways to these higher emotions.

The Mental Body

Your Mental Body facilitates the logical and left-brain functions and sees itself as the 'real you' or the ego. It will, if allowed to, control much of your mundane life believing that it exists in 'fight or flight' world. When you enable the creative right brain's ability to receive and express your heart's higher emotions you can directly access the wisdom of the Universe in which it is always and innately connected to. This is why following your heart is often times smarter than what you think.

The Spiritual Body

Your Spiritual Body is the divine essence or spark of life that vibrates at the frequency in which to animate and express through the current three-dimensional paradigm of our physical world. This is but a small aspect of your Soul and is focused on this current life in which you are living in this specific perceived dimension of time and space.

Your Spiritual Body connects all of the other body systems together through the primary energetic centers called the Chakras. When each Chakra, or energy center is clear, balanced, vibrating at its optimum frequency, and in coherent alignment, you are in harmony with yourself and the world around you.

The Soul

Your Soul is the greater aspect of who you truly are. It is the culmination of all of your lifetimes experienced in all dimensions of time and space and is the higher essence and expression of your innate divinity. It is objective and determined it its pursuit to learn, grow, expand and evolve to ever-increasing higher frequencies of expression, experience and existence. You can catch glimpses of it through deep meditation, or in moments of Divine inspiration, Bliss and Joy. You will know it when you experience it, as you will feel and recognize it at every level of your being. You will know that you are a part and connected to everything in the Universe.

"Connecting to who you truly are will show you exactly where your Soul wants to go."

15

Passion Filled & Purpose Driven

If you are not living your purpose, you'll be living by default, feeling lost and confused. Connecting to who you truly are will show you exactly where your Soul wants to go.

Therefore, it is critically important for you to understand what you want to accomplish in your life, as early as possible. This is not something you leave until a certain pre-determined age, as the sooner you figure out why you are here and what you've planned to achieve, the sooner you'll be on your way to creating the life that you truly want.

As an adult, and if you want to remember what your life purpose is, you'll want to spend some time working through the steps. A life worth living is a life well lived. And, a happy and fulfilling life is one lived with great passion and purpose.

Each step to creating the life that you want is broken down to practical daily exercises that will by virtue create your new Energetic Immune System along the way. Practice makes perfect, and as the days fly by, you'll be that much closer to living the life you want. So, start by living in the moment with the conscious realization that you've just taken the most important first step in creating the life that you not only desire, but the one you are destined to live.

1. Get Connected ~ Take time in your daily meditation to connect through your Crown Chakra. Doing so will improve your connection to Unity Consciousness and your Higher Self. The results will be a clear vision of your true purpose in life and a deeper connection to who you truly are. *Feeling connected is priceless.*

2. Be Inspired ~ Spend time in your meditation and tap in through your Third Eye Chakra for inspiration and visualizing the life you want to consciously create. Or set aside a weekly appointment with just you and your imagination and

see where it takes you. Your Third Eye Chakra is also the gateway Chakra to your innate Intuition. *Your imagination isn't something you give up once you grow up.*

3. Be Expressive ~ Getting the words out right can be a challenge. Whether in your relationships at home or at the office. Keeping your feelings and emotions pent up can cause energetic blocks at the Throat Chakra ~ which will only create bigger issues in your life. Solve this energetic challenge when you take fifteen minutes a day to write your thoughts and feelings in a journal. You will improve your clarity and focus while also move through your emotions for effective communicating. *Effortless expression spells happier relationships.*

4. Follow Your Heart ~ Live your life from the heart with love, compassion and gratitude. Start your day expressing gratitude for everything and everyone in your life and you'll see abundance of every kind increase in your life. Feelings are the energetic magnets of life, and when you feel gratitude

through your Heart Chakra, the Universe has only one option to answer with more good stuff for you to feel grateful for. *Feel the gratitude baby.*

5. Be Masterful ~ Manifesting in your life requires an inspired idea, clearly expressed; some heart focused magnetism and then energized through your manifestation portal, the Solar Plexus Chakra. Become the creative master in your life when you take five minutes each day to send out an emotionally charged power ball to manifest what you want in your life. Get it down with practice, trust your gut instincts and see your creative seeds take root and begin to grow in your life. *Become the creative master of your life.*

6. Be Yourself ~ Sex is a beautiful and natural part of life. Keeping your Sacral Chakra balanced and humming is critical. Spend just a few minutes a day clearing out the energetic debris from sexual tension, frustration or imbalance from an overloaded Sacral Chakra. Excessive sexual stimuli can tip this Chakra out of balance and create an

unhealthy imbalance in the entire Chakra System. *Honor your sexual expression and create a balanced body energetic.*

7. Grounded Passions ~ Grounding your body to Mother Earth through the Root Chakra is essential for feeling passionate and full of sustainable vitality in your life. Take ten minutes every day to feel the Earth beneath your feet without anything in between. The electromagnetic energy from our planet directly harmonizes with our energetic blueprint through the Root Chakra. Sit under a tree, take a walk on the beach or simply plant your bare feet on the grass to reconnect and recharge yourself with the life-sustaining energy from Nature and Mother Earth. *Get grounded.*

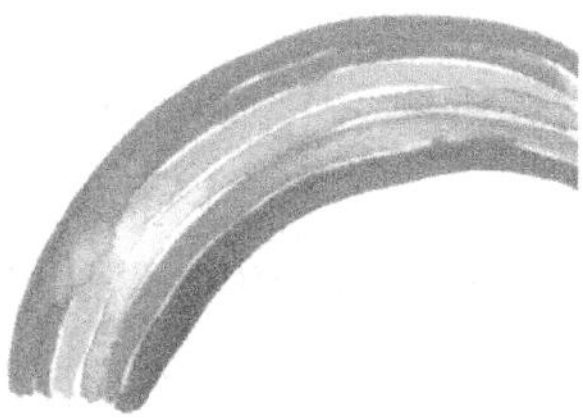

"Imagine a world without the color purple and you've just painted the world grey."

16

Your Rainbow Soul

Each Chakra's energetic frequency resonates within the spectrum of Light. And just like a rainbow, your life is also created and supported by the Sun's rays, the air you need to breath, the water that you are mostly made of while you are physically connected to Mother Earth.

Our physical body, along with every other mundane and invisible aspect that makes up the human experience is a creation of the Universe that exemplifies the 'As Above, So Below' expression.

Connecting to Mother Earth through our feet on the ground is similar to planting a seed in the ground. And, just like that seed, we also need her life force in order to grow and thrive. Aside from all of the essential foods that she provides in the way of nutritional support, her energetic frequency also supports us.

The Chinese mapped the body's energetic grid system they call the Meridians thousands of years ago. Used with great success for healing over the past five thousand years, this energetic freeway system that supports our body to function in a cohesive and at nearly instantaneously speeds reaches its own connection point where it meets the ground.

And, just like the grounding point of the Chinese Meridian Systems, The Root Chakra is also at the ball of our feet and is the entry point for Mother Earth's energy into the human field of energy.

Earth's electromagnetic field has been measured in frequency and was originally discovered by German scientist Winfried Otto Schumann. Commonly referred to as the Schumann Resonance, Earth's pulsating electromagnetic field resonates at 7.83 Hertz.

This is the same optimal frequency that the human body's electromagnetic field functions at. This harmonic resonance of Earth's 7.83 Hz frequency and its correlation to the human body has been shown in double blind studies, and in practical applications to have definite positive results with many health disorders.

The human brain in a healthy state has also been shown to oscillate at 7.83 Hertz. As such, our brains function and are in a natural state of resonance with Earth's electromagnetic frequency.

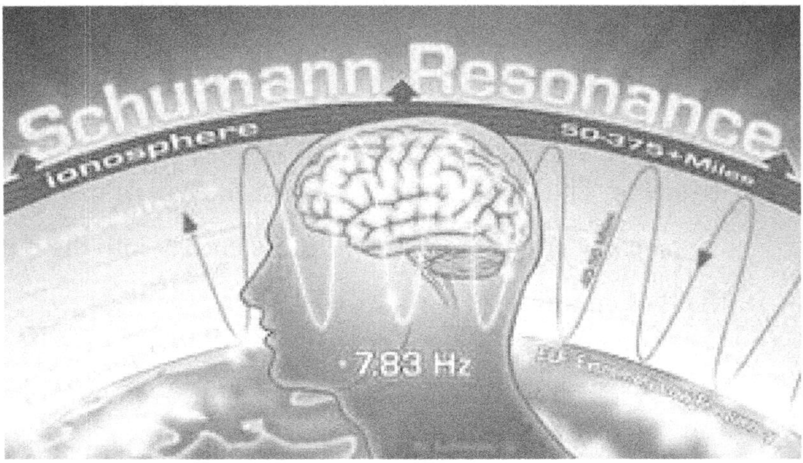

If you've ever experienced jet lag, you'll find it easy to understand how our body becomes adversely affected when we are flying 30,000 feet above the ground. The cause of jet lag is much more than simply traveling across time zones. Not only are we physically disconnected from Earth, but we also become energetically disconnected from Earth.

When astronauts returned to Earth physically and mentally exhausted from their first ventures into space, their resulting "space sickness" was a mystery. Eventually, researchers discovered that unlike Earth, space lacks a magnetic field. Their solution was to create the essential harmonic frequency of the Earth's magnetic field for the astronauts while they were in space.

In addition to energetically grounding our body to Earth in order to maintain harmonic resonance for optimum health, Earth's energy supports us with the vitality and passion we all want to feel in our lives. The color red in the light spectrum field, while not always visible to the eye, is the color of Earth's vitality and energetic field. The correlation of her life-giving energy as it directly relates to the color our human blood is of no minor coincidence.

Any time you want to create something in the physical world, you need to combine the energy of the Divine Feminine Spirit with the Divine Masculine Spirit. When you are creating a new life, you will energetically do this through the sexual and reproductive Sacral Chakra.

Combining these two energies of the Divine Feminine energy from Mother Earth and your connection to her through your Root Chakra's red frequency, along with the Divine Masculine energy from the Sun's rays and your connection to it through your Solar Plexus Chakra's yellow frequency results in a focused creative force to create a new life through the Sacral Chakra's Orange frequency light spectrum.

Mix the colors yellow and red and you'll always get orange. We live in a creative Universe where energy is light vibrating at different frequencies within the limitless creative electromagnetic spectrum that our world is created from and functions within. The active combination of the lower three Chakras are always required to create and manifest on the physical plane, whether at the conscious or subconscious level.

The saying 'follow your heart' often falls on deaf ears because we've been trained to live our lives through logic and a self-limiting perspective based on the five physical senses. However, walk into any deep green forest, and it takes barely a moment for you to begin to feel what this truly means.

Your heart is the center of your Universe and when you physically connect with Nature, you will feel a palpable sense of calm and serenity come over you with almost immediate results. It should appear obvious to you that the color your heart innately resonates to is within the frequency spectrum of green.

Balance and centering in your everyday life can easily be achieved and maintained by spending regular time in and surrounded by Nature. It is a holistic experience for the body, mind and spirit.

Now you are immersing yourself not only through the five mundane senses, but also on an energetic level. Consciously connecting to Nature through your Heart Chakra is an absolute necessity to living with peace and serenity in your life, but also an important key to living the life that you truly want and are destined to live.

Expressing your life through your thoughts, feelings and emotions, whether they are spoken or written down, energetically moves up the light spectrum of resonance through the Throat Chakra. While sound and the spoken word carries an energetic force that can bind the creative power of the Universe due to its vibrating at a higher frequency, expression at this level will by virtue connect you to the higher levels of expression in your life.

Earth's waters physically appear at the same frequency and in a wide color range. From the Amalfi coast's beautiful aquamarine to the deep dark blue of the Pacific Ocean, Earth's watery expression is an undeniable connection for everyone.

Whether you are emotionally inspired or captivated when physically near water or not, we express ourselves, our creativity and our thoughts, feelings and emotions through our own bodies that are also made up of mostly water. It is another direct connection to Mother Earth that we can easily overlook and take for granted.

When we are emotionally overwhelmed, stressed or upset, why do we want to take a hot shower or treat ourselves to soaking in a hot bath? And how do you feel afterwards? Natural Hot Springs, thermal waters and going to a Spa are all water-based cleansing experiences that can release tension and relieve stress at the physical, emotional, mental and spiritual levels.

According to H.H. Mitchell, Journal of Biological Chemistry 158, the brain and heart are composed of 73% water, while the lungs are made up of around 83% water. The skin contains 64% water, the muscles and kidneys are 79%, and even the bones contain a watery 31%.

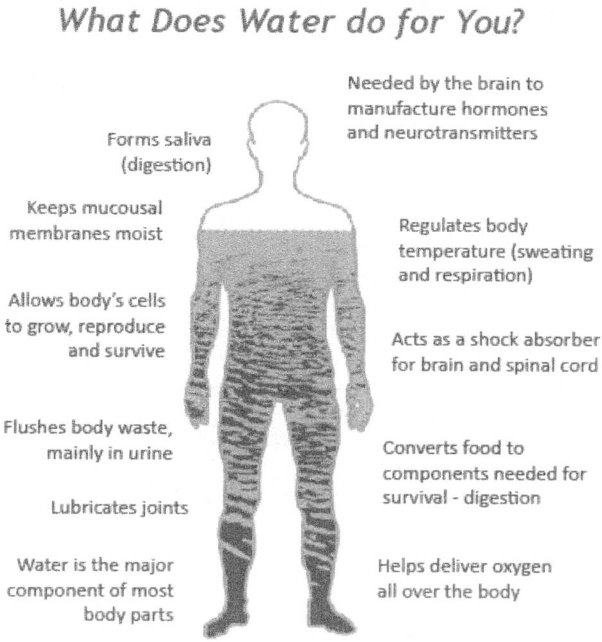

Each day humans must consume a certain amount of water to survive. Of course, this varies according to age and gender, and also by where someone lives. Generally, adult males need about 3 liters per day while an adult female needs about 2.2 liters per day. You can live longer without food than you can without water.

As we move up the frequency spectrum, living your life without feeling inspired will leave you without a reason to live. Everyone wants to feel inspired about life. Imagine a world without the color purple and you've just painted the world grey. Any first grader knows that you can't make purple without mixing red and blue together. Shades in between can be created with tints of yellow along the way, and so it also is within the light spectrum of living our lives.

Divine inspiration then comes through a grounded connection to your passions and vital life force from Mother Earth, and then accessed through your Third Eye Chakra. This is your higher intuition and access to divine inspiration from the higher frequencies of the creative Universe's energy field.

The 'As Above' part of the creative equation is referring to the divine inspiration that can be experienced through the Third Eye energetic frequency of indigo or purple light spectrum. If you want to create something from divine inspiration or tapping into your imagination you will access it by tuning in through this frequency station.

You'll feel in tune and connected your inner visionary guidance system when you meditate or simply get quiet and close your eyes to ponder your life. Sitting under a tree or surrounded by Nature while visually appreciating nature's beauty will also get you vibrating in the violet frequency spectrum. This is yet another way to directly connect to

Earth's harmonic resonance to feel a part of life's bounty, beauty and limitless potential to create in your own life.

"Your subconscious mind is the software to your hardware. Program in equals program out. No matter what your conscious mind will want on the outside, your life is first created at the energetic level."

17

What Color are You Living?

If your Energetic Immune System is out of alignment on the inside, your life will show you on the outside. We live in an energetic Universe that never sleeps. You too are an energetic being that is always on the move, even while you sleep.

Aspects of your energetic body will rest at night, while the essence of who you truly are will remain active, aware and connecting at a higher level within the collective field of consciousness to help resolve inner conflicts at the energetic level.

And, when you are awake and moving through your day, you are taking in and expressing energetic patterns every step of the way. So, you'll want to make sure that your energetic immune system is in alignment. You'll also want to be sure that your individual energetic blueprints have been created from a conscious level rather than by default. By default, means that they have been subconsciously created from old subconscious habits, beliefs or patterns you learned along the way.

By the same token, and unless you energetically protect your field of energy, you'll also be susceptible to other people's energetic blueprints that you come in close contact with. Your heart's field of energy can extend out from your physical body for as far as *twelve to fifteen feet*, so you'll want to also understand how to energetically protect yourself so as not to pick up unwanted energy from others.

Let's start at the beginning with these two aspects of energetically expressing yourself in your life and how to consciously become aware of how to live from your energy rather than from someone else's.

Everyone comes into their new life with a plan of what they want to learn and achieve. Whether you are a believer in reincarnation or not, is not important. Only that you begin to understand that this life of yours and the world in which you live is a life is designed by the creative power of the Universe. And within that is a grand design that includes you in the plans.

Therefore, your life and what you accomplish along the way impacts each and every one of us at a collective level.

While you may be living from a conscious level most days, most people will unconsciously pick up beliefs and programs from their parents, siblings, and environment during the early years of their childhood.

From birth to around ten years of age, you are energetically open and susceptible to picking up these beliefs, patterns, and habits ~ whether healthy or not, at an energetic level from those you are around the most.

You are being conditioned and grow up in an environment that shows you how to live your life, both from an energetic level through subconscious programming as well as your environmental conditioning.

Now you can easily see why you may be acting like your mother or father more than you consciously would like to. Although you may be consciously aware of these unwanted behavioral patterns and beliefs picked up from your family conditioning, until you create a new blueprint to replace the old ones, you will continue to play out the old subconscious programs.

Your subconscious mind is the software to your hardware. Program in equals program out, no matter what your conscious mind will want on the outside, your life is first created at the energetic level.

The key to living the life you want, instead of repeating someone else's habits and beliefs, is to first identify what's truly yours and what you want to keep in order to live the life you want.

Parental influences are not the only early life influences that can sway you from your true purpose in life. The media has also become a huge player in early childhood subconscious programming through television advertising for the toy, video game and fast food industries.

Along with cartoons, music and movies, children today are systematically exposed to recipes for subconscious programming from a young age in order to create tomorrow's consumer.

If you are a parent, you can use this information to help protect your child from unwanted subconscious programming. And, instead provide an open and supportive environment that encourages your child to remember from an early age what they are here to do.

If most parents asked their son or daughter this question while they are under the age of six, their child would probably tell them exactly why they are here. It might as simple as; I'm here to teach you how to love again. Or, I don't want to be afraid any more.

Life doesn't need to be complicated, but we tend to make it more so than even we'd like it to be sometimes.

"Feeling connected is priceless."

18

Connecting the Dots

I Connect - Connecting through Your Crown Chakra
Feeling connected is priceless.

Your Crown Chakra is the doorway to your Soul and can give you the perspective of the Universe at large and your place within it. This is no small thing, and while it may seem lofty and ideal to many, it actually has a fundamentally critical purpose in your everyday life.

That purpose is to help you gain a greater perspective on your unique and individual role within the grand plan and scope of the evolutionary process at large. It will also enable you to remember, recognize, and realize at a very down to earth practical level your true life's purpose.

Remembering why you are here now at this critical moment in humanity's evolutionary process is one of the most important things for you to do now. Remembering who you truly are will reveal by its very nature, your true purpose in life. And, as each one of us remembers our true purpose in life, we step one soul closer to creating a more beautiful world for everyone.

Along with remembering of who you truly are, you will also remember why you are here now. It's crazy time on Planet Earth right now. So how on Earth could this be a good thing for you to be here now?

No other time in humanity's history has life been more polarized and full of chaos on a global level. There is no country or culture that is not currently experiencing some form of upheaval, conflict and chaos. While the pendulum continues its swing of extremes, you have the unique and rare opportunity to experience more, and yet at the same time to remember, recognize and realize who you truly are.

That may seem even more unlikely, yet the opposite is true. No one makes much progress when the skies are blue, and the sun is shining. People tend to make the necessary changes in their lives only once they are forced due to sheer desperation or dislike for their current circumstances. It's just human nature.

The last piece of the puzzle in remembering who you truly

are and why you are here now, is to realize what you are to do next. This is the 'aha' moment when you see the pieces come together and the puzzle of your life up until this very moment start to fall into place. There is a great sense of relief in this moment when your Soul immediately recognizes that everything before this has led you to right here and right now.

This is one of the most perfect moments a person can experience in their lives, and you will know it when you experience it. So, you can see that connecting through your Crown Chakra to the greater aspect of who you truly are, is of the utmost importance.

Not only to your life, but to Humanity's evolutionary process as well. This is the why and how one person does make a difference. It is also why we can't do it without you. And what you've come here to do in the unique way that only you can do it.

Without knowing who you truly are, and what you want to create, you will live your life by default, or defined by someone else's idea of what you 'should' be doing, and how you 'should' be living your life. You will be living your life without a compass and be tossed about like a boat lost at sea.

Once you've remembered who you truly are, why you are here now and what you are to do next, you will be on your way to creating your new Crown Chakra Energetic Blueprint and on your way to living your life full of passion and purpose.

Get Connected

Take ten minutes a day to connect through your Crown Chakra. Doing so will improve your connection to Unity Consciousness and your Higher Self. The results will be a clear vision of your true purpose in life and a deeper connection to who you truly are. *Feeling connected is priceless.*

Symptoms of an under-performing Crown Chakra:

You are unsure of your true purpose in life, you feel unfulfilled, disconnected, lost and confused in your life. Or, you may know exactly why you are here, but are unsure or afraid of how to begin living it. In addition, you could also feel your connection to your Higher Self so much, that you aren't fully grounded to your everyday life.

Crown Chakra Solutions:

Integrate a daily meditation to connect to your Higher Self.

Create a clear intention for connection. Once you remember who you truly are, you will naturally begin to realize why you are here now, and then what you came here to do next. Wear the Crown Chakra gems and integrate the Crown Chakra I Am Prayer into your daily life.

Crown Chakra Support Tools:

Colors: White, Ivory, Clear Crystal

Gems: Quartz Crystal, Diamond, Moonstone

Element: Higher Self/Unity Consciousness

Flowers: Jasmine, White Lily

Aromatherapy Essential Oil: Frankincense, Lavender, Cedarwood

"Your imagination isn't something you give up once you grow up."

19

I Realize - Connecting through your Third Eye Chakra

Are you inspired in your life, or lacking a visionary view?

Without a clear view of what inspires you in life, you will be living your life with blinders on. Or worse, living someone else's idea of what you 'should' be doing and how you 'should' be living.

The next step in creating the life you want will be to open and access your Third Eye Chakra. Everyone is born with his or her Third Eye Chakra open and fully functioning. However, many children gradually disconnect from it when they are encouraged to think more than actively engaging their imagination.

Whether your parents shunned your creative side in preference to academics or other 'more practical' pursuits are of no concern, as it's never too late to regain your very important inner visionary world.

The Third Eye Chakra is your gateway to what I call your Inner Visionary Guidance System. This Inner Visionary Guidance System is made up of three essential elements: your Innate Intuition, Imagination and Divine Inspiration.

Your Innate Intuition is your inner guide to navigating your life in those moments when you need to know which way to turn, left or right, or continue straight ahead.

Your innate intuition will let it be known through that little voice in your head, visionary dreams, déjà vu, sudden strong feelings that something feels right, or make a quick left and avoid disaster ahead.

Often times, you'll ignore these little or not so little inklings, and later recall that you had fair warning. These are all opportunities to show you to pay closer attention to your trusty Intuition, as it will always guide you safely through any storm.

Like any workout in order to keep in shape, there are some great exercises you can do to improve your Innate Intuition. I include several intuition exercises in my workshops and retreats. You can find out more on my website to help you if you want to get your Intuition in great shape.

The next essential element in your Third Eye Chakra is your Imagination. It is also one of the most over looked and underappreciated assets you have in your Chakra Toolbox. Accessing your Imagination through your Third Eye Chakra is absolutely critical to creating the life you truly desire. Without having a vision of where you want to go, how can you possibly create the life you want?

Your imagination isn't something you give up once you grow up. Whether you want to create an entirely new life from the ground up a new career, relationship or simply make some necessary adjustments here and there, there are some fundamentals you will want to know.

The ground rules of life you weren't taught in kindergarten are however the cornerstones of your new life. Before creating your new life, you will want to clear any energetic blocks or self-sabotaging behaviors. It requires a review of the current emotional triggers, programs and scripts you've learned along the way.

You may have some lingering or long-held beliefs, thought patterns, or emotional memories from your relationships. They can originate from family patterns, everyday exchanges to life-changing trauma. If you are prone to excessive criticism, suppressed anger, ongoing frustration, long held resentments, projection of self-loathing to self-hatred, the good news is that there's no need for a long drawn out process or rehashing painful experiences and memories. You simply need to replace the old patterns with new energetic blueprints that are consciously created by you, the true creator of your life.

The key is to identify the patterns playing out in your life and then work through the process of releasing and then creating new energetic blueprints from the inside out.

The truth is that while events can change lives for better or worse, the emotional baggage can be checked but not claimed at any point.

Most people experience their life and the world in which they live trusting, relying and believing that reality exists based on the physical evidence that the five basic senses show them. However, quantum physics shows us that when the observer is present, their observation of the particles impacts their behavior and affects real change.

This means that as we engage and observe in our own lives, we directly influence our perceived physical reality at an energetic level. So, you will want to engage your imagination and begin creating your reality from this place before you ever begin to expect your life on the outside to show any improvements.

Along with imagining your new and improved life, you'll want to engage the emotional experiencing aspects in order to add the magnetic attraction required to actually manifest it into your new life.

The third element that makes up your Third Eye Chakra is accessing Divine Inspiration. This is where you get that idea or inspiration to create or invent something new, otherwise known as the Universe's field of limitless divine creative force, from which all creations arise.

This is the field of limitless possibilities that anyone can access at any time. This is the reason why multiple people will invent something similar within a short span of time, yet live continents apart.

We live in a creative Universe and everything that you can see, feel, touch, smell or hear has been created by someone who has simply accessed their imagination, tapped into this limitless field of creative energy and followed their new idea through to completion. Whether it's Beethoven's Fifth or Michelangelo's David, all of this and more is possible without limits when you use your imagination and access your right to create from this place.

You, me and everyone else in this world are the divine creator in our own lives, and with global potential to change the world, one person at a time. Never, ever underestimate your imagination and the power to create something new. It just may be the next great idea ~ or you may inspire someone else to create something of divine proportions.

You may never know how you've made a real impact in the world at large – so never give up on an idea that you feel inspired to create. It could change your life or the world for the better.

Combine these three essential elements by supporting your Third Eye Chakra and you can easily see how important they are to create the life your heart truly desires. There is limitless power here for you to access and utilize in creating a powerful Third Eye Chakra Blueprint leading to the life you desire and deserve. Use it wisely.

Your Third Eye Chakra Toolbox:

Get Inspired ~ Your imagination isn't something you give up once you grow up, but a valuable asset to feel inspired in your life.

Spend 5 minutes in your meditation and tap in through your Third Eye Chakra for inspiration and visualizing the life you want to consciously create. Or set aside a weekly appointment with just you and your imagination and see where it takes you. Your Third Eye Chakra is also the gateway Chakra to your innate Intuition. Learn to trust your Intuition and you'll never go wrong.

This is the Chakra that you can access your inner visionary guidance for your everyday life. It is also the source for divine inspiration and is the greatest source for creativity through your imagination. It is where you can tap into the Universes' limitless creative force. Tapping into the power of this Chakra is also the source of your innate intuition.

It is that voice that gives you hints and clues when you need to turn left or right in your life. Consider your intuition your 'Inner Visionary Guidance System' to guide you through your life. Once you learn to trust your innate intuition, you won't go wrong.

Envision your life exactly the way you want it to be. You must know how you want your life to look like from the inside first. This is setting the visual blueprint of what your life will look like on the outside once it comes into form. Engage your imagination, get inspired and experience how it will feel to live the life you truly desire.

Take your time and get it just the way you want it. If you have chosen to experience life at a certain level in order for your Soul to learn something, then you will realize it at this stage in the creative process. If you try to imagine living in a huge mansion, but it doesn't feel right, then this is not what you've come here to experience in this life.

By the same token, if you imagine a nice comfortable house in a new city that you would love to live in, and that feels right, then you'll know you're coming into alignment with what is in harmony with your Soul's plan.

This is not to say that you should diminish what you want to create, but only as an example of separating fantasy from what's in your highest and best interest. And, this is why it is critical that you get your new life vision exactly the way you want it and that it feels right to you. If that big mansion feels right, then go for it.

This step is critical to getting it right and the way that feels right to you from the inside. This is not about fantasizing, but sincerely imagining how you want your daily life to be like at every level. See it and emotionally experience each area of your life the way you really want it.

Symptoms of an underperforming Third Eye Chakra:

You feel a lack of inspiration in your life or a disconnection from your inner visionary guidance. You tend to mis-read people and their true intentions, which can lead to deception. You have a difficult time making decisions in your life and tend to overreact rather than respond with balanced instincts and perspective.

Third Eye Chakra Solutions:

Integrate a daily meditation and practice using your imagination to get inspired about your life. Also practice the 'Inner Genie' exercises with friends and family to hone your innate Intuition. Wear the Third Eye Chakra gems and integrate the Third Eye I Am Prayer in your daily life.

Pure Inspiration Mantra:

Connect to the limitless Universe for divine inspiration and illumination. Feel the ideas that illuminate and elevate you to a new level of life. Allow your Inner Genius to reconnect with your conscious mind and begin to feel inspired again.

Third Eye Chakra Support Tools:

Colors: All shades of Purple, Lavender

Gems: Amethyst, Tanzanite

Element: Air

Flowers: Iris, Freesia, Violet and Lavender

Aromatherapy Essential Oil: Lavender, Clary Sage

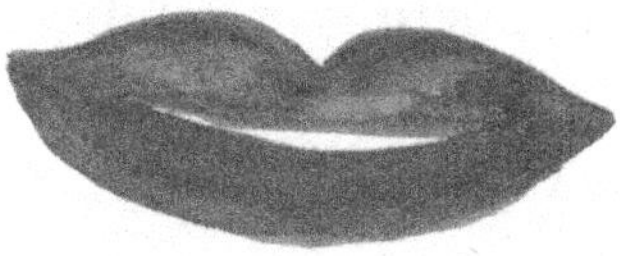

"Whether in rage or with a whisper, every word you speak carries an energetic vibration as it leaves your mouth and reverberates out into the world around you."

20

I Express - Connecting through your Throat Chakra

Are you expressing yourself fully, or are you holding back?

Unless you are fully expressing your thoughts, feelings and emotions, you'll be missing out and tripping over opportunities to grow and experience fulfilling relationships.

The next Chakra is one in which many find challenging, as the Throat Chakra is the gateway to expressing yourself within your everyday life and the world around you.

The Throat Chakra when energized and in balance, offers you the freedom of expression to engage with your friends, family and associates at every level of life. The key to fully express yourself through the Throat Chakra is to keep it all in balance, with clarity and focus.

The Throat Chakra plays a special role in that it is the primary Chakra for communication and expression of every thought, feeling, and emotion. Whether sweet or sour, with passion or poison. Your voice with the world, whether spoken, spit or written is your megaphone of your life to the world around you.

Do you use your Throat Chakra effectively and with grace, compassion and love? Or with clear intentions to do damage, wreak revenge and retaliation?

Here is where getting your lower Chakras in check and balance will directly affect how you communicate in every area of your life. While we're putting the cart before the horse a bit, it is essential for you to fully understand the power of the spoken word. Whether in rage or with a whisper, every word you speak carries an energetic vibration as it leaves your mouth and reverberates out into the world around you.

Your words will carry the venom or antidote within them and directly impact its recipient with your consciously intended, or 'unintended (baggage-carrying) impact. Thinking before you speak is always a great idea, but often becomes a concept lost on ideals when you're in the heat of the moment.

Also, to be noted, is that the health of your Energetic

Immune System will be greatly impacted from your lower three Chakras when they contain old patterns of behavior, emotional trauma, and memories. These old patterns of behavior, emotional traumas, and memories can also get stuck in your Energetic Immune System and inhibit you from fully expressing yourself ~ sometimes for an entire lifetime.

These are the types of emotional stresses that can also wreak havoc in your life and potentially become the root cause for developing chronic health issues. Even to the extent of eventually manifesting life-threatening diseases. Medical research studies show, over and over again, that stress, which is caused by highly charged emotional experiences and traumas, cause *upwards of ninety percent of all known major diseases.*

Holding on to the past does more harm than good in our lives, and in every way. Our emotions are there to help us experience the enormous range of experiencing the beauty, joy, and love in our lives. They are designed to be experienced, moved through, learned from and then let go of. The problem for many is that they hold on to these emotionally charged memories and replay them over and over and over again, whether in their minds, in their relationships or on their therapist's couch.

If you are feeling depressed in your life, there is an emotional element that needs to be recognized and then released. The only reason for long-term depression is that you do not understand how to move through your emotional experiences and then let them go. Reliving unhappy past events that keep a hold on you to the point of becoming depressed is simply a matter of repetition and nothing more.

Your emotions are there to provide you with a platform of experiential contrast, wherever it may fall within the spectrum of emotions. Good, bad or indifferent, your emotions create a backdrop for reflection and learning. Wisdom can evolve out of one's greatest moments of fear, conflict and unhappiness.

The key is to understand that each emotion that you experience along the way is meant to be short-lived and not held onto. You want to ride your emotional highs and lows like a rollercoaster ride. Enjoy and experience the dips and peaks for what they are, and then move on. You cannot stop at the top of the climb and relish the feeling of anticipation any more than you would want to stay at the bottom with your stomach still in the air. Life is intended to be a rich adventure, filled with experiences that you will not only enjoy and treasure, but also learn from.

Once you've been through a difficult experience and felt the sense of loss, disappointment, hurt or betrayal, why would you ever choose to constantly repeat and relive those feelings? Recognizing that there is always something of value for you to learn through every type of emotional experience will give you a new perspective on your life.

And learning how to experience your life with thoughtful reflection along the way, and then letting go of what no longer serves you will provide a backdrop for wisdom as you go.

Getting stuck in the spectrum of so-called negative emotions is the cause of long-term depression. And, learning how to let go of the past and what you cannot change is the solution to regaining your emotional equilibrium.

When you are aware and consciously creating each part of your life, you will no longer let pieces of it slip through the cracks and back into subconscious patterns. Each area of your life is a part of the whole, and it is with forethought and planning that you can begin to build a fine-tuned and effortless flow of abundance into your life.

Emotional freedom offers you the opportunity to create the life you want from a conscious level. And that means that you will not be creating from the past, or from your subconscious default system. Within your subconscious lay the ancestral patterns, childhood traumas and early-life belief systems that will not serve you well in life.

Therefore, you will want to create with focused intention and expressed with thoughtful clarity through your Throat Chakra. The power of the word cannot be overstated, as this is one of your greatest assets to creating and manifesting your life.

The power of the spoken word carries your clear intentions into the Universe's mixing bowl of ingredients. Speaking and saying out loud what you are intending to create propels your ideas, goals and desires out and into the energetic web of creative mix with tremendous power and force.

Thoughts also carry energy and add to the formula, but with limited force and energy. Therefore, you will want to integrate the power of the spoken word into any project or creative desire you are looking to manifest.

The importance of having a clear and balanced Throat Chakra is of the utmost importance. You will want to keep it functioning at optimal performance by making a conscious effort to clearly express yourself at every level, and in every area of your life.

Take your time when expressing yourself. And take the time to consciously think about what you want to say, rather than emotionally reacting in the moment. This can be easier said than done; however, practice will go a long way to helping you to perfect this aspect of your life.

When you are feeling emotions rise from the gut level and emotions start to charge the conversation, take a conscious step back and take a deep breath. Ask yourself why you're getting emotional and be willing to take responsibility for allowing your buttons to get pushed.

The other person may be saying things that you don't like to hear, and whether true or not, it is always your choice on how to respond. Reacting from an emotional place is not going to help you to express yourself with clarity.

More than anything else, pent up, repressed and long-held emotional resentments can keep you from expressing yourself, clearly and with focused forethought in your life.

This unfortunate aspect of having a Throat Chakra that is blocked, over-stimulated or otherwise underperforming, will greatly restrict your ability to create fully in your life.

The key to creating a healthy, balanced and open Throat Chakra is to live in the moment, to be present and neither look to the past to define who we are, for the what if's, if only's or could have been's.

When creating your new Throat Chakra Blueprint, you'll want to keep it to yourself until you've got all of your Chakra ducks lined up, clear and energetically clacking along in a single file resonance of harmonious ducky-ness.

Your ability to clearly expressing your heart-centered visions, desires and dreams in your life and with the world, is an absolute essential Energetic Blueprint for success, health, happiness and fulfillment. There will be no getting around this one. *Clear communication is the key to happier relationships.*

Your Throat Chakra Toolbox:

Be Expressive ~ Getting the words out right can be a challenge. Whether in your relationships at home or at the office. Keeping your feelings and emotions pent up can cause energetic blocks at the Throat Chakra ~ which will only create bigger issues in your life.

You are capable of creating anything that you desire. You are a limitless creator living in a limitless creative Universe. You are capable of creating your life exactly the way you want it to be, as long as it is in direct alignment with what you have come here to experience.

This is the Chakra for expressing yourself through the spoken word. It is also an important power center for creating anything you want in your life. The power of the spoken word sends out a frequency wave of energy to set the new creative blueprint to the Universe. When you combine your heart-felt emotions with your spoken word, the force and impact will be felt on the level of intention that you speak it.

This is why it is so important for your Throat Chakra to be balanced and functioning properly. So, you will want to choose your words with forethought and send them out with the emotions that you want to respond with, rather than react from.

Symptoms of an underperforming Throat Chakra:

You are often misunderstood, argue often, or feel defensive, make excuses or feel the need to justify your actions and feelings. You tend to use the wrong words or react with too much emotional emphasis. Or you are not fully expressing how you truly feel, repressing your thoughts and emotions to the point of resentment.

In addition, you may be quick to point the finger and blame others. All of these issues come from an underperforming Throat Chakra with additional under-performing Chakras that are contributing to these symptoms.

Throat Chakra Solutions:

Integrate a daily meditation and begin keeping a daily meditation journal. The next step in the creative process is to begin to express your new visionary blueprint through writing everything you want down in your journal to help reinforce your new life design. In complete privacy, say the I Am prayers to set the energetic blueprint with the power of the spoken word. Until you have moved through all of the steps to setting each Chakra Blueprint, keep your new creation to yourself.

This will protect you from others trying to rain on your creative parade. Remember that this is your life, therefore you are the master creator of it, so you don't need others permission, input or approval of your new life blueprint.

Often times, it is our closest friends and family members who will be the last ones to be supportive. Everyone wants to feel the love and support from loved ones in their life, especially when creating something new.

However, you must also understand that when it comes to creating your new life, you are the only one that needs to believe in you. And, sometimes people need to see it first, before they can be supportive. So, show them what you are made of and be an example that will inspire those around you that they can also become the masterful creators in their own life.

If you are having communication issues at home or at work, take the time to write down all of your thoughts, feelings and emotions that come up around those issues. Even if it sounds petty, judgmental and you feel the need to play the victim, you still need to express and move through those emotions. Writing it down will help you to regain your emotional center around the issue and you'll come to see the challenge as an opportunity to learn something about yourself.

Relationship issues are never about one person, but an opportunity for both people involved. Effortless expression spells emotional release, which will result in happy and healthy relationships.

Also practice the Clearing Your Throat Chakra exercises to release and clear the energetic blocks. Wear the Throat Chakra gems and integrate the Throat Chakra I Am Prayer in your daily life.

Pure Expression Mantra:

Connect to your Inner Voice and let the world hear, see you, support you and love you. You are here to be recognized and appreciated for your unique contribution that only you can make.

Throat Chakra Support Toolbox:

Colors: All shades of Blue and Aquamarine

Gems: Aquamarine, Iolite, Kyanite, Apatite, Amazonite

Elemental: Water Sprite

Element: Water

Flowers: Blue Delphinium, Hyacinth

Aromatherapy Essential Oil: Basil, Bergamot, Chamomile

"This amazing organ that we often times ignore, neglect, and build walls around, is where we can find our greatest strength, our faith, our courage and our compassion, enabling our higher emotional intelligence that can, if we allow it, guide us throughout our lives."

21

I Am - Connecting through your Heart Chakra

Are you living from the heart, or with the barricades up?

Living from the heart without the walls and defenses constantly up and ready for battle will open you up to the world and life that is full of love, acceptance and fulfilling connections. Love makes the world go 'round. Get on board.

Much like a gyroscope, your Heart's energetic field is the center of your Universe yet connected to everyone and everything in the world around you. It is from this heart-space that you want to navigate your life from. From the most mundane to the highest ideals you hold within, creating, living and experiencing from your Heart is what living a life of passion and purpose is all about.

Holding this heart-centered balance will require some concentration and focus until you create a solid and steady seat for your higher visions and goals to be created from.

To begin creating your life in this way, you may want to start at the beginning and rewrite some programs.

The goal is to heart-center respond rather than emotionally react. When you are living from your Heart, your ego will no longer be sitting in the driver's seat. And, when you begin to live from the heart, you will leave the fight-or-flight reactionary self in the back seat where it belongs.

Your physical heart is an amazing organ, unique for both its physical functions and energetic properties, and therefore needs some extra special attention, and definitely some tender loving care.

Your Heart Chakra is the center-point of the Chakra system for very good reason. Your physical heart is the center of your Energetic Universe, and mine, along with every other living being, creature, ant and atom in existence.

Aside from the fact that the heart is the first major organ to develop in the fetus after conception, it is also impossible to live without one beating brightly within each of us. In addition, the heart's ability to tell us when we fall in love, experience joy, feel gratitude, and appreciate beauty, it is without question, the tour de force for our passions in the pursuit of happiness and fulfillment throughout our lives.

While these statements are nothing new, Neuro-physicists have recently been astonished to discover that the Heart is more an organ of intelligence, than merely the bodies' main pumping station.

These new discoveries include intriguing evidence that more than half of the Heart is actually composed of neurons of the very same nature as those that make up the cerebral system. Not only that, but the heart also emits a *5,000 times stronger electromagnetic field than the brain.*

Joseph Chilton-Pearce, author of The Biology of Transcendence, calls the heart "the major biological apparatus within us and the seat of our greatest intelligence." In an interview from a 1999 issue of JOURNAL OF FAMILY LIFE magazine, Mr. Pearce explains how this 'heart-brain' functions:

"The heart responds to messages sent to it from the emotional brain, which has been busy monitoring the interior environment of dynamic states such as the emotions and the auto-immune system, guiding behavior, and contributing to our sense of personal identity.

The emotional brain makes a qualitative evaluation of our experience of this world and sends that information instant-by-instant down to the heart. In return, the heart exhorts the brain to make the appropriate response. Of course, all of this is on the non-verbal level”.

According to the Institute of Heart Math, "the heart and brain maintain a continuous two-way dialogue, each influencing the other's functioning. The signals the heart sends to the brain can influence perception, emotional processing and higher cognitive functions. Neuro-cardiology researchers view this system and circuitry as the "heart brain". In a comment regarding intuition, HeartMath goes on to say,

"Heart intuition or intelligence brings the freedom and power to accomplish what the mind, even with all the disciplines or affirmations in the world, cannot do if it's out of sync with the heart."

The HeartMath Institute has also conducted additional research relating to our emotions, which they call, "Emotional Energetics Research" and publish the following statement on their website:

"The heart produces by far the body's most powerful rhythmic electromagnetic field, which can be detected several feet away by sensitive instruments. Research shows our heart's field changes distinctly as we experience different emotions. It is registered in people's brains around us and apparently is capable of affecting cells, water and DNA studied in vitro. Growing evidence also suggests energetic interactions involving the heart may underlie intuition and important aspects of human consciousness."

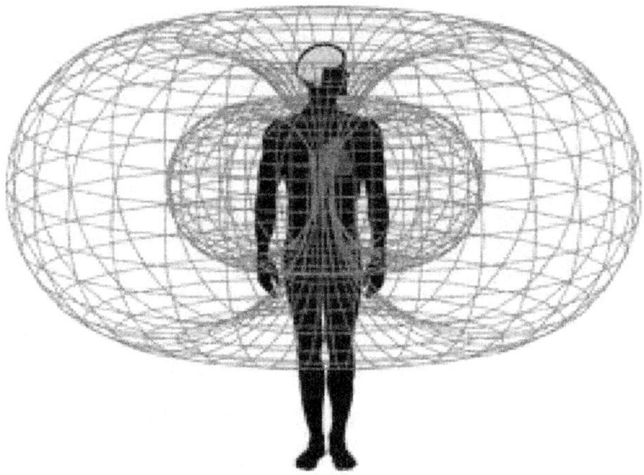

Copyright Institute of HeartMath Research Center

This next bit of news is one of the most interesting, as the geometric shape that the Heart's electromagnetic frequency creates - is in the form of a torus field.

Similar to the shape of a donut, the heart's torus field

radiates out from the chest for as far as twelve to fifteen feet from the body. The axis of this Heart torus extends from the pelvic floor to the top of the skull, and the whole field is holographic, meaning that information about it can be read from each and every point within the torus' energetic field.

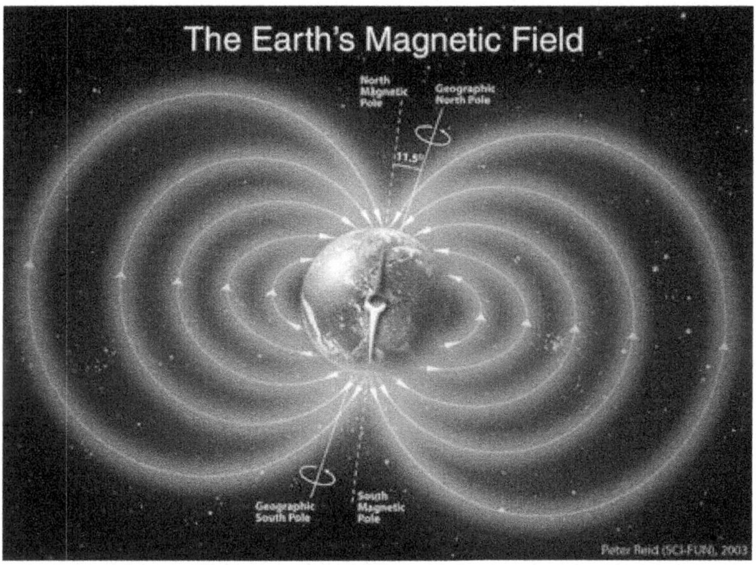

Even more intriguing is that the Heart's torus electromagnetic field is not the only physical source that emits this type of electromagnetic field. In fact, all atoms emit the very same energetic torus field. Earth also emits

its own electromagnetic field in the same form of a torus. So does each planet in the solar system, and even our galaxy. And *all are holographic*.

Scientists believe there is a very good possibility that there is actually only one Universal torus encompassing an infinite number of interacting tori within its spectrum. And, because electromagnetic torus fields are holographic by nature, it is more than likely that the sum total of our Universe is present within the frequency spectrum of a single torus.

This means that each one of us is connected to the entire Universe, in a very real and observable way. As such, each one of us has access to all of the information within this Universal field of energy, at any given moment. When we get quiet and access what we hold in our Hearts, we are literally connecting to the limitless supply and wisdom of the Universe, thereby enabling what we perceive as "miracles" to enter into our lives.

This amazing organ that we often times ignore, neglect, and build walls around, is where we can find our greatest strength, our faith, our courage and our compassion, enabling our higher emotional intelligence that can, if we allow it, guide us throughout our lives.

Other branches of Science are also confirming with substantial evidence that the responses the heart makes, affect the entire human system, and in significant ways.

Molecular biologists have also discovered that the heart is the body's most important *endocrine gland.* Our hearts actually produce and release a major hormone, ANF (Atrial Neuriatic Factor) in response to emotional stimuli, which profoundly affects every operation in the limbic structure, or what is referred to as the "emotional brain." This includes the hippocampus area where memory and learning take place and is also the control center for the entire hormonal system.

A published research article by Adolfo J. de Bold in the University of Ottawa Heart Institute goes on to say; “It is now well established that the atria of the heart in mammals including man, produce two polypeptide hormones: microscopy atrial natriuretic factor (ANF) (13) and brain natriuretic peptide (BNP) so named because it was first detected in the brain) (8). Thus, these cells are involved in both the mechanical activity of the atria and the endocrine function of the heart.”

Quite literally, we have another "brain" located in our heart. And, through the same type of neurotransmitters, it is linked to every major organ and muscle in the body.

Additional Research from The Institute of HeartMath

The Institute of HeartMath Research Center has been conducting research for over nineteen years and is a recognized global leader in emotional physiology, optimal function, resilience and stress-management research. The center conducts research into psychophysiology, neurocardiology and biophysics, and frequently collaborates with universities, research centers and health-care-system partners. Their research has significantly advanced our understanding of heart-brain interactions, heart-rhythm coherence, and the physiology of optimal learning and performance.

The HeartMath Institute also conducts research studies to include the electrophysiology of intuition and exploring how we are all *globally interconnected at a deep, fundamental level via electromagnetic fields and biofields through our Heart*, which they call, “Emotional Energetics Research”.

HeartMath also includes Neurologist Antonio Damasio’s

research results on their website. Author of Descartes' Error, Dr. Damasio emphasizes the importance of emotions in the decision-making process: "*He points out that patients with brain damage in the areas of the brain that integrate the emotional and cognitive systems can no longer effectively function in the day-to-day world, even though their mental abilities are perfectly normal.*"

In the recent bestselling book Emotional Intelligence, Daniel Goleman argues, *"that the pervading view of human intelligence as essentially mind intellect is far too narrow, for it ignores a range of human capacities that bear equal if not greater weight in determining our successes in life"*.

The latest research in neuroscience is confirming that while we each possess two unique systems of intelligence; the key is to integrate the thinking mind with the heartfelt emotions into a coherent and balanced system in order to live up to our optimum potential. It is also interesting to note that while there is a clearly demonstrated two-way dialogue between the brain and emotions, the actual number of neural connections going from our emotional centers to the cognitive centers is greater than the other way around. This last bit of information clearly explains the tremendous power of our heartfelt emotions.

The Symphony Your Heart Plays

When researchers looked a little closer at the Heart's unique and newly discovered properties and functions, an even more astonishing discovery was revealed. Each heart cell is unique in that it not only pulsates in synchrony with all the other heart cells, but also produces an electromagnetic signal that radiates out beyond the cell.

An EEG that measures brain waves shows that the electromagnetic signals from the heart are so much stronger than brain waves, that a reading of the heart's frequency spectrum can be taken from three feet away from the body, *without the need to place electrodes on it.*

Additional HearthMath research goes on to show that once we have an emotionally-charged experience, it can create an 'emotional blueprint' for future behaviors, affecting us in our daily lives, our attitudes about our life, and even impact our life time achievements.

Our emotions can also "bump mundane events out of awareness, but the non-emotional forms of mental activity like thoughts do not so readily displace emotions from the mental landscape".

And in the same way, our experiences act as reminders for our most repetitive and habitual thoughts, which are the very thoughts that are actually fed by our most intense emotional experiences.

HeartMath goes on to state, "Because emotions exert such a powerful influence on cognitive activity, at IHM we have discovered that intervening at the emotional level is often the most efficient way to initiate change in mental patterns and processes. Our research demonstrates that the application of tools and techniques designed to increase coherence in the emotional system can often bring the mind into greater coherence as well.

It is our experience that the degree of coherence between the mind and emotions can vary considerably. When they are out-of-phase, overall awareness is reduced. Conversely, when they are in-phase, awareness is expanded. This interaction affects us on a number of levels: Vision, listening abilities, reaction times, mental clarity, feeling states and sensitivities are all influenced by the degree of mental and emotional coherence experienced at any given moment".

This emerging scientific evidence has the enormous

potential to open the minds of anyone willing to stop long enough and reflect on what this truly means to each and every one of us. Not only are we discovering the true potential of every individual should they begin to live from their heart, rather than solely from their logical mind, but also to fully grasp the truth that we are all intimately connected and collectively one.

Your Heart and mine are not only connected through this intricately woven web of energetic blueprint fields, but they are affecting us all in unseen ways, yet impacting us in ways that can and do make a difference.

As this new science of the heart so clearly demonstrates, what we say, do, think and feel not only creates our individual energetic blueprints, but also coalesces into a collective Universal Energetic Blueprint, thereby creating the world in which we are living our lives. It is the quintessential example of the microcosm within the macrocosm.

Now is a perfect moment to stop and take a closer look inside of yourself and see what you are contributing to the current collective blueprint of our world. You may find some terrific new thoughts, actions and deeds that you are consciously creating. You may find a combination of some great contributions along with a dash or two of fear-based, blame-focused, competition-fueled, or scarcity-inspired paradigms running through your energetic immune system as well.

No harm, no foul. Just take a peek and make the necessary adjustments. Really, you'll be doing all of us a great favor by being honest and coming into conscious alignment with anything that is out of harmony with what your heart truly wants.

Remember that this is the Chakra that connects you to everyone and everything in the Universe through Torus field of energy created by the physical heart. This is *the* power center that connects to everyone and everything in your world. It is the center of your Universe. This is the point when you will be setting your new life blueprint in your heart and the world around you.

If you have done your previous work well, this is when you will begin to feel a deep inner knowing that what you are creating is in direct alignment with what your true heart desires. You will feel it anchored in your heart, and this is when you know you are creating something that is worthy of your time, energy and focus.

When you are living from the heart, your life will be in balance and harmony. The Heart Chakra is also where we experience our feelings and create the higher emotions: Love, Compassion, Joy, Bliss, and Gratitude. Appreciating your life, beauty, art, music, your loved ones, and connecting with Nature and all living creatures is experienced and expressed through the Heart's energetic field.

Connecting to your Heart will allow you access to your 'Inner Genius'. Your Inner Genius is where you tap into the wisdom of the Universe and the higher frequency of Universal Love.

Setting your Heart Chakra blueprint is the single most important step you will take, so if something doesn't feel quite right, make the necessary adjustments at this point. Life is not a stagnant experience, but an ever-evolving adventure. You'll be evolving right alongside of what you are creating, so go with flow and know that you'll see things differently as you move through creative process. What you thought you wanted yesterday may not be something you want today.

Setting your Heart Chakra Blueprint will also be where faith and trust come into place. As once you set your new blueprint, you'll want to feel complete faith in what you've chosen to create, along with trusting that the Universe will now bring about the synchronistic events, connections, resources and people to bring it into form.

Included in setting your Heart Chakra Blueprint is feeling Gratitude for all that you have right now and right here. You want to express that gratitude daily and from your heart. Also feel grateful for your new life as if you are already living it. Feel the gratitude for everything you've envisioned and expressed with the knowing of how it feels to you at every level.

It is critical that you get your Emotional Experiential Quotient, or EEQ, right at this juncture. The stronger you express your feelings of experiencing your new life as if it's already happened, the faster you will set your new Heart Chakra Blueprint into the Universal Blueprint for accelerated creation.

Gratitude is also the energetic gateway to experiencing Joy, Bliss and Ecstasy in your life. You can consciously create a state of Joy through simply focusing on it from the Heart Chakra. Experience Bliss when you go into a full state of appreciation for Beauty, and Ecstasy when you combine the two. Live with great gratitude and love in your life and you will touch and inspire others in unseen ways and help change the world in the very best of ways.

As each one of us begins living from our Heart, we will begin to see it reflected in our lives and in the world. It is also how each one of us will create real and lasting change in our personal lives, and as a direct result, also create a new and better world in the process. This time truly is the quiet revolution of the heart and why the Heart Chakra is the center of your, and my Universe.

Your Heart Chakra Toolbox:

Follow Your Heart ~ Live your life from the heart with love, compassion and gratitude. Spend five minutes a day feeling grateful for everything and everyone in your life and you'll see abundance of every kind increase in your life. Feelings are the energetic magnets of life, and when you feel gratitude in your Heart, the Universe has only one option to answer with more good stuff for you to feel grateful for.

Follow your Heart for heart-centered living and watch your life overflow with improved health, increased wealth and abundance of every kind. *Feel the gratitude baby.*

Symptoms of an underperforming Heart Chakra:

You will feel sad, depressed, disconnected from others and the world. You may be experiencing health challenges, feel frightened and scared of life in general. You may also feel hopeless and despair, or feel like the victim of your fate, and without control in your life. Hate may be a word you use often and see others as the enemy rather than an ally.

You rarely feel grateful for all that you have in your life. You may feel a lack of compassion and understanding for other's struggles in life. You tend to grab what you can out of life for yourself with little thought given to sharing or helping others in need.

Heart Chakra Solutions:

Integrate a daily meditation and start by feeling grateful for everything and everyone in your life. Each day look around you and feel appreciation for all of the beauty in the Nature and the world. Also practice the Heart-Centered exercises with friends and family to open and balance your Heart Chakra. Wear the Heart Chakra gems and integrate the Heart Chakra I Am Prayer in your daily life.

Pure Balance and Serenity:

Connect to your Heart and enter the serenity that resides within. Feel the inner wisdom you hold within knowing that no matter what is happening on the outside you are always safe and secure on the inside. Balance is the key to calming the mind, body and spirit.

Pure Health:

Connect to your Inner Healer and feel the innate balance come back into alignment with you, body, mind and spirit. Let go of the frustration, anger and judgment you have been holding within. Forgive yourself and forgive others. Feel the tension release its hold and feel the renewed sense of freedom to be happy again. Be gentle with yourself, within and with the world around you to allow spontaneous healing and renewed health to be restored.

Pure Prosperity:

Reconnect with your Inner Genius to restore your ability to receive. Take the golden key you hold within and open the door to Prosperity you have kept locked for so long. Open your Heart with a great sense of relief at the renewed feeling of Gratitude you feel for the great prosperity in your life now. Let go of the worry and frustration of not having enough. Connect to the limitless Universe's supply of great Prosperity knowing you are always safe, secure and with more than enough in your life.

Each morning and night remember to give Gratitude for all that you have in your life. Say "Thank You, Thank You, Thank You" for your perfect health, wonderful and loving family, friends and new opportunities coming into your life now.

Heart Chakra Support Toolbox:

Colors: All shades of Green and Pink

Gems: Peridot, Emerald, Jade, Green & Pink Tourmaline, Rose Quartz, Rhodochrosite, Kunzite

Elemental: Faerie

Element: Air

Flowers: Lotus, Orchid, Rose

Aromatherapy Essential Oil: Rose, Jasmine, and Lavender

"Manifesting in your life requires an inspired idea, clearly expressed with heart centered energetic magnetism and then energized through your manifestation portal, the Solar Plexus Chakra."

22

I Transform - Connecting through your Solar Plexus Chakra

Are you creating abundance, or struggling to just get by?

Struggle and financial lack happen when you energetically turn the abundance tap off. Financial success is the direct result of the Universe responding to your conscious ability to create it. Open the abundance faucet to your life, and get the money flowing again.

Without the Sun, no life on Earth could survive for very long. With the sunrise, a new day dawns, and as the sun sets, another day comes to a close somewhere on Earth. So, it is with our Solar Plexus Chakra. While our hearts are filled with great desires and passions, the job of our Solar Plexus is to bring those dreams and desires into reality in our lives and out into the world.

Manifesting in the mundane world is the primary function

of our Solar Plexus, however manifesting doesn't happen all at once. Like all living things that grow in our world, there are specific requirements for the healthy production of even the tiniest of things.

There are basic elements that contribute to manifesting anything into your physical reality. From seed to plant, conception to birth or design to product, each requires the necessary ingredients in order to develop, grow and emerge in your life, and the world around you.

First and foremost is the idea or concept and that will have sprung from your intuition, inner visions or divine inspiration. The second comes from expressing the idea through your thoughts, plans and words. The third required element is what the Heart adds by connecting the energetic dots, with the force equal to the heartfelt passion and desires you feel. These three elements must be in harmonious alignment before you will be ready to take action, action, action.

Now you will need to bring it all through the Solar Plexus and add the energetic blueprint from the Sun while grounding it to Mother Earth. Combining these two energies with your creative vision comes together and sets your new energetic blueprint. You've created something new and have given it an *electromagnetic* charge of its own.

The electrical charge comes from the concept, thoughts and words, while the magnetic pull or attraction is created from the feelings and emotional desires you've added from the heart. Some call this electrical part the Law of Attraction.

However, as you've probably already discovered, creating is not simply 'attracting' what you think you want. When you learn to consciously create what you desire following the Universal Law of Creation, your life will transform into the life you truly desire.

You've created something truly unique. Now you need to get out of your own way and allow your new energetic blueprint to ripple out and connect you to the synchronistic events, people and resources to manifest it into your reality and the world.

This doesn't mean to say all hands off and there's no further action needed by you. You will need to know in an unwavering and concrete way, that you have created this new energetic blueprint, and that there can be no questioning about the when, or how it will come into being. No doubts, no fears and no insecurities are allowed if you want an easy and seamless creative process.

All endeavors worthy of great success require time, patience, research, hard work and diligence. If you've created your new energetic blueprint from a truly heart-centered place, and your individual energetic blueprints are all in coherent alignment, it will by virtue of the Universal Law of Creation, have to manifest. That is, unless you give up.

Now it's the job of the collective Universal Blueprint to 'fill your creative order' energetically. It's like going through the drive-through window; sometimes there are cars ahead of you and you have to wait a bit.

Remember that the Universe always delivers at the right time, and the right place, and in the highest and best interest of you, the creator. Here is where many people get caught up, so stay open and flexible as the Universe can work in mysterious ways, but it is always on your side.

As you continue to do the things you need to do along the way, don't be surprised if there are adjustments and revisions you make on your own. Life is a creative process, and sometimes you decide to paint with different colors. The point is to paint your life canvas with all of the colors and creativity you can muster.

Creating from your Solar Plexus will also give you direct feedback through those gut instincts you feel along the way. Whether they are butterflies or danger signs, always pay attention and make any necessary adjustments along the way.

Your Solar Plexus Chakra Toolbox:

Be Masterful ~ Manifesting in your life requires an inspired idea, clearly expressed with heart centered energetic magnetism and then energized through your manifestation portal, the Solar Plexus Chakra.

Become the creative master in your life when you take five minutes a day to send out an emotionally charged power ball to manifest what you want in your life. Get it down with practice, trust your gut instincts and see your creative seeds take root and grow in your life. *Be the creative master of your life.*

Once you have your vision aligned with your emotions, you

will set your Solar Plexus Chakra Blueprint in the world around you through your actions. This point in the creative process requires you to take the necessary actions to achieve your new life.

Regardless of what it is, your physical participation is now required. With the faith and trust you felt in your Heart Chakra; you now need to take action every day to connect your Solar Plexus Blueprint to your physical world.

This is where the lower emotions come into play, so trust your gut instincts and follow the clues that the Universe will now send you. Whether those clues come in the form of new people, something you come across in a magazine or synchronistic events, pay close attention during this phase.

The Solar Plexus Chakra also directly connects you to the Sun's powerful and life-giving energy source. The sun is the embodiment the Divine Masculine Spirit. The Divine Masculine Spirit is the active ingredient in creation, whether you want to conceive a baby, or start a new project. This is the energy source that when combined with the Divine Feminine Spirit has the creative potential to create anything in your life.

Follow through in every way that you see or discover is also critical during this stage in the creative process. This is the interactive play in the mundane world that you will need to actively participate in to see your new life emerge around you.

The Universe works in mysterious ways but will always respond by filling your new blueprint orders. It may manifest in a different time frame than what you want, but patience will always pay off. So never give up on your dreams, or on what you have created at an energetic level.

Remember that this is the Chakra that you create your life from. It is the Chakra that you live your daily life through in the mundane world. If you want to manifest financial wealth, career success, a new car or that new house, you will want to learn to use your Solar Plexus Chakra for its creative potential.

Tapping into this Chakra requires connecting to your outer physical world with the creative force of the Universe that is powered by the Sun's energy. Without the Sun's energy, no life can exist on Earth.

Therefore, when you are creating something you want, you will also need to tap into the limitless power source of the

Sun. Think of the Sun as the Divine Masculine Spirit, and Mother Earth as the Divine Feminine Spirit. This is simply done by balancing your Solar Plexus Chakra so that it is not overly active.

Symptoms of an underperforming Solar Plexus Chakra:

You'll know if this Chakra is out of balance if you are experiencing financial struggle in your life. This is where it becomes extremely important to recognize any belief or habitual patterns that you may have picked up along the way. You may also have a tendency to emotionally overreact with a low functioning Solar Plexus.

By the same token, if your Solar Plexus is underperforming in your life, you may have shut it down due to a lack of connecting with the physical world around you. Feeling a great sense of limitation and scarcity in your life will also constrict the Solar Plexus Chakra. Also, if you are living from a dominantly fear-based perspective, you will be limiting your potential to actively create what you want in your life.

Solar Plexus Chakra Solutions: Integrate a daily

meditation and emotionally envision what you want your life to be like. Engage the emotions with a great sense of relief because if feels great to finally have all that you want in your life again. Feel it and experience it with a great sense of gratitude. Exhaling with great relief that your life is finally back on track.

Practice the Solar Plexus exercises to open and balance your Solar Plexus Chakra. Wear the Solar Plexus Chakra gems and integrate the Solar Plexus Chakra I Am Prayer in your daily life.

Solar Plexus Chakra Support Tools:

Colors: All shades of Yellow and Gold

Gems: Citrine, Yellow Sapphires, Honey Jade

Elemental: Fire Salamander

Element: Fire

Flowers: Sunflower, Daffodil, Dandelions

Aromatherapy Essential Oil: Lemongrass, Sandalwood

"Bringing the Sacral Chakra into balance will have you experiencing your sacred sexual bliss again through an aligned body, mind and spirit."

23

I Energize - Connecting through your Sacral Chakra

Are you experiencing your sexual joy or feeling frustrated and unfulfilled?

The beauty of your sexuality is more than what the eye beholds, but an expression at every level. Bringing the Sacral Chakra into balance will have you experiencing your sacred sexual bliss again through an aligned body, mind and spirit.

This is the Chakra that functions for reproduction purposes and creating a new life from. It is the Chakra that you express your sexuality through. Experiencing a healthy and balanced sex life is achieved through a balanced and open Sacral Chakra. Energetically connecting with another person through the Sacral Chakra can open you up to experiencing states of pure Bliss when all of your Chakras are in balance along with practicing conscious Sacred Sexuality.

The art of sexual union has a higher energetic purpose; which can enable you to access pure states of Bliss, rather than fleeting moments of mere physical pleasure. When you bring your awareness and conscious intention of sharing who you truly are with your partner through your Heart Chakra you will open the gateway to a state of whole body ecstasy and you will begin to feel the love of their true Heart.

Imagine what it would feel like to connect with him/her at every Chakra: you know who they truly are, and they in turn know and see you for who you truly are. Connecting to their inner beauty with your inner vision will begin to integrate the energetic connection of true beauty and will disconnect you from experiencing your union through the limited physical senses.

Through your energetic blueprints, you are connected ~ body, mind, heart and spirit. This is why you want to choose your sexual partners with great care. Even if your conscious awareness is only at the physical experiential level, you are still opening yourself up - at every energetic level to your partner's energetic blueprints.

If you aren't already, begin integrating the view of your sexuality and the intimacy of energetically connecting with another as a sacred form of sharing yourself at every level. This is a great way to bring greater balance and alignment to your Sacral Chakra.

Your Sacral Chakra Toolbox

Be Yourself ~ Sex is a beautiful and natural part of life. If you want to create a new life, or simply want to have a healthy sex life, keeping your Sacral Chakra balanced and humming is critical. Spend just a few minutes a day clearing out the energetic debris from sexual tension, frustration or imbalance from an overloaded Sacral Chakra.

Exposing yourself to too much sexual stimuli can tip this Chakra out of balance and create an unhealthy imbalance in the entire Chakra System. *Balance is the key to this Chakra for a healthy and satisfying sex life.*

Symptoms of an underperforming Sacral Chakra:

You'll know if this Chakra is out of balance if you are experiencing an overly active sex life or feel sexually repressed and unfulfilled. You may also have lost your connection to Sacred Sexuality through energetic distortions by being visually desensitized and over-stimulated by watching sexually explicit videos.

This can also contribute to becoming bored and unfulfilled in your sex life. At an energetic level, everyone instinctively knows that there is much more to sex than the physical act of a pleasurable experience. You may also experience sexual dysfunction, fear of emotional intimacy, infidelity or overly needy.

Sacral Chakra Solutions: Integrate a daily meditation and emotionally envision your heart-centered partner. Engage the emotions with a great sense of peace and tranquility of finally connecting on all levels with the perfect partner for you now. Feel it and experience it with a great sense of gratitude.

Practice the Sacral exercises to open and balance your Sacral Chakra. Wear the Sacral Chakra gems and integrate the Sacral Chakra I Am Prayer in your daily life.

Sacral Chakra Support Tools:

Colors: All shades of Orange

Gems: Carnelian, Mandarin Garnet, Songea Sapphires

Elemental: Water Sprite

Element: Water

Flowers: Bird of Paradise, Marigold, Tiger Lily

Aromatherapy Essential Oil: Orange, Cardamom

"If you want to manifest anything in your life, you will also want to ground your creative ventures to Mother Earth. "

24

I Emerge - Connecting through your Root Chakra

Are you living with passion or feel disconnected and alone?

Feeling a lack of passion and vitality in your life can be a direct result of isolating yourself from Nature. Connecting to Nature energizes you with the sustaining vitality of Mother Earth's harmonizing energetic vibration with your body, mind and soul.

Once you've started to interact on a physical level with your new life, you will want to ground yourself to Mother Earth through the Root Chakra. Connecting to Mother Earth also provides the energy of passion in your life. It comes from the harmonic resonance of your body connecting to hers.

Look around you and appreciate the beauty of nature that surrounds you and see if you don't feel a great sense of passion for your life. Spend time in nature and connect yourself and your new cohesive and aligned blueprints to the ground beneath your feet.

You receive Earth's energetic frequency she emits directly to your energetic body system. If you want to manifest anything in your life, you will also want to ground your creative ventures to Mother Earth. The Root Chakra is also how you can renew or ignite the energy of passion in your life.

Grounding your physical body to Mother Earth can also transmute the stress and strain of living a busy life. Feeling gratitude for this beautiful and magnificent planet on which we walk, sleep and live our lives, can bring great energetic release and healing of the stress, angst and strain of having a tough day.

If you feel overwhelmed, go for a walk, meditate under a tree, ponder the blue sky, or rescue a bug from a puddle. The next time you hear a bird sing, stop and listen, really listen to the incredible beauty that surrounds you. Escape from the daily rat race and spend time with the trees that live in your back yard or down the street. Trees are really great listeners and they won't judge you.

If you live in a large city, pot some flowers or an herb garden to sit on your windowsill, or start a community garden in a nearby empty lot or patch of unused ground. Beautify your life with nature, and nature will sooth your soul back to a grounded and passionate place.

Also realize, that our beautiful planet is being systematically stripped of her natural resources. So, do whatever you can to make all of the little shifts in how you live your daily life to reuse, recycle and reduce the waste your life creates. Buy fewer products in plastic and begin making your own personal care products from natural ingredients. It will be healthier for you and for our planet.

The resources today abound for living in harmony with nature in order for all of us to thrive into the new world we are collectively creating, one person at a time.

Think of it this way; if every person you know, and then all of the people that they know started to integrate a conscious effort of living a life in harmony with nature, how quickly our world would change for the better? It's the hundredth monkey effect. Except that we aren't monkeys. Go out and plant those feet on the ground outside or sit under a tree. Now start to imagine your perfect world. What would it look like?

Now bring that passion for the planet that provides you with all that you need and more and bring it into your heart. This is where the better world for everyone begins. With you and me. Practice makes perfect. Always remember, that a life worth living is a gift that requires visionary heart-felt passion.

Earth is much more than most perceive her to be. Mother Earth is the embodiment of the Divine Feminine Spirit in action. Therefore, remember that if you want to create anything new in your life, you'll want to ground yourself and connect to her creative power as well.

Like the egg, Mother Earth possesses the creative power of all new life. It is she who provides the ground, water and air that sustains all life in combination with the Sun's life sustaining energy. You cannot create with only one half of the creation equation.

Also, when you spend time getting to know who Mother Earth truly is, you will also come to remember what that truly means to you. You'll be amazed and surprised. I know I was.

Your Root Chakra Toolbox

Grounded Passions ~ Grounding your body to Mother Earth through the Root Chakra is essential for feeling passionate and full of sustainable vitality in your life. Take ten minutes every day to feel the Earth beneath your feet without anything in between. The electromagnetic energy from our planet directly harmonizes with our energetic blueprint through the Root Chakra. Sit under a tree, take a walk on the beach or simply plant your bare feet on the grass to reconnect and recharge yourself with the life-sustaining energy from Nature and Mother Earth.

Remember that this is the Chakra that you receive Earth's energetic frequency she emits that directly resonates with the human body. If you want to manifest anything in your life, you will also want to ground your Solar Plexus Chakra creative ventures to Mother Earth. The Root Chakra is also how you connect to Nature and can receive the energy of passion in your life. *Live a passion filled and purpose driven life.*

Symptoms of an underperforming Root Chakra:

You'll know if this Chakra is out of balance if you feel out of touch with your surroundings and feel a lack of passion in your life. If your Root Chakra is underperforming in your life, you may have shut it down due to a lack of grounding with nature and Mother Earth. Feeling afraid and spending too much time inside can also constrict the Root Chakra.

Root Chakra Solutions:

Integrate a daily meditation and begin to spend time out in nature appreciating the beauty that surrounds you. Go for walks or practice Yoga on the beach, in your back yard or in a beautiful park. If you live in an apartment or big city, fill your house with plants and fresh flowers. Start an herb garden on your windowsill or balcony.

Feel and experience the immense beauty of Nature with a great sense of gratitude. Practice the exercises to open and balance your Root Chakra. Wear the Root Chakra gems and integrate the Root Chakra I Am Prayer in your daily life.

Root Chakra Support Tools:

Colors: All shades of Red

Gems: Ruby, Garnet, Deep Pink Tourmaline

Elemental: Gnome

Element: Earth

Flowers: Red Roses, Poinsettias

Aromatherapy Essential Oil: Frankincense, Oakmoss

Those are the fundamental steps in the creative process called your life. If you want to accelerate your new creations manifesting in your life, incorporate the I Am Prayers on a daily basis along with supporting each Chakra by wearing natural gems and crystals for added energetic support.

"The stronger the emotion, the stronger the energetic ripple to the point of building up into a wave that can come crashing down upon the shores of your life today, tomorrow or years down the road."

25

Your Emotional Quotient

Ever since I was a little girl, I could sense what others were thinking and feeling. Even today I can go back to a major event in my life and feel the emotions of the experience. Everyone can do this. Emotions are stored in our memories and emotions have an energetic blueprint of their own.

Big or small, emotions can leave a lasting imprint on your life. For an entire lifetime if you allow it. While re-experiencing happy and joyful moments might be something you'd like to do every now and then, holding onto emotional trauma, grief and sadness is not good for your soul, or your life in the long run.

Like everything in our Universe, all human emotions have an energetic signature unique to you and your life. And each emotion you experience goes out from you like a ripple in the sea. Whether you can see it or not, it is nevertheless there. And the stronger the emotion, the stronger the energetic ripple to the point of building up into a wave that can come crashing down upon the shores of your life today, tomorrow or years down the road. The key to not creating emotional tsunamis in life is to learn how to move through your emotions with heart-centered grace.

How do you do that when someone in your life has done something to make you upset, hurt or angry? Nine times out of ten, those people in your life have not consciously intended to cause you hurt or pain but have made a choice to speak or act without considering anyone else but themselves in the moment.

While I'm not trying to remove responsibility, I am simply pointing out that once you grasp this fundamental fact of human nature, you can take a step back and see the bigger picture.

Once you can truly appreciate this, then you can begin to move into a more heart-centered perspective in your own life. This simply means, that you open your heart up to understand that everyone is on his or her path in life. In addition, this also means that you will never fully understand another's perspective and choices in how they choose to live their life. And, therefore it is not for you to judge.

When you begin to see that trying to fully understand how someone else thinks and feels in making their life decisions is an impossibility, you will come to appreciate their unique contribution and that this is part of what makes life so interesting and fun.

So, when you find yourself in an emotionally charged situation, how do you stay in your heart centered space and not emotionally react? While I won't say it's always easy, or necessarily possible in every situation, the more you come to understand your own emotions, the easier it becomes.

Why can't someone else feel the same way as you in the moment of conflict or argument? Simply because they are not you and don't see things from your perspective. So, the sooner you let go of that expectation of how others live their lives; the easier things will be for you in your own life.

The first key to establishing your emotional center is to meditate. The reason for this is because meditating brings you back to your heart center. And once you are in your heart you will not be pulled down into the lower emotions so easily. You will also begin to gain more compassion rather than judgment of other's lifestyles and choices.

Living from your heart gives you the big picture view that we're all here to experience a wide range of what life has to offer from our own unique perspective.

Once you begin meditating on a regular basis, you'll begin to feel and see your life from a broader perspective. You will also feel more centered, balanced and calm. The little things in life will not bother you so much, and petty grievances will not hold your attention for as long as they once did.

The second key to maintaining your heart-centered balance is to learn how to experience your emotions as they ebb and flow without creating a permanent and emotionally charged energetic blueprint.

When conflict arises in your life, deal with it and move on. Your emotions are not intended to be replayed over and over like the latest hit song on the radio. Who wants to listen to the same song over, and over and over again? The problem for many people is that they replay the emotional drama over and over again in their minds and hearts.

And this is where the danger comes in that you will begin to create a negatively charged energetic blueprint in your life. And this is how we create self-sabotaging patterns that keep us from realizing our dreams and living up to our greatest potential.

One of the biggest reasons people replay their emotional traumas is to justify that they have been wronged and are therefore a victim. Woe is me, someone done me wrong they say. These individuals are looking for hopeful sympathy and attention from others rather than understanding that there is always, and I mean always, an opportunity for greater understanding and growth in their own life through these experiences.

The other big reason is that they truly don't know what do to with these powerful emotions and they get stuck in them. In our modern society today, we still haven't created a healthy education on how to deal with and express our emotions. And, unfortunately, sometimes we learn our worst emotional habits from our parents and family situations.

So, what do you do if you are one of these people who has grown up to be just like their mother, or father? The good news is that although you've become good at creating negatively charged emotional blueprints, you can also rewrite those blueprints with new positively charged blueprints.

The third key to grounding your heart-centered life is to bring your awareness up to where you can be totally honest with yourself about how you emotionally react in moments of conflict.

Do you immediately engage by going on the offensive and attack, or do you get highly defensive and make excuses? There are many variations on these themes; the key is to be honest with yourself, so you can begin to change the reactionary behavior.

Once you fully recognize your emotional identity on the scale of reactionary to responsive, you can begin to create new positive emotional blueprints.

Let's say you are feeling a little depressed about something that's happened in your life. Nothing major, but it's got you feeling down. Why do you feel this way? Because something has happened that you didn't want to happen. The purpose of your emotions is simply telling you that you want to change the situation.

So, what can you do to change it? If you can't change what happened, you can certainly change how you feel about it. And this is where you begin to learn that all emotions are meant to be experienced and short-lived. Then you look for the gift, the lesson or the Universe's 'redirect' sign and get going back up into the positive energy spectrum.

Now you take steps to move out of the emotions by taking your attention off of the sadness and begin to create positive energy in your life again. No point in wallowing as that will create a stagnant energy and you're not here to do the same thing over and over again, right?

There are easy and simple ways to shift out of feeling the blues that will have you bounce back faster and create a positive vibe again in your life. You can very simply 'lift' yourself out of the negative energy spectrum by removing any and all negativity from your life. And then you will ADD as much positive energy to your life.

Watch a funny movie and laugh till your belly aches. Another great way to create a positive energy shift is to write a list of everything you are grateful for in your life. Put on your favorite dance music and dance around your house. Or if you can't go there just yet, put on some soothing music to help neutralize your mood while you write your list of gratitude.

Another wonderful way to shift your energy out of depression is to go outside and sit under a tree and appreciate all of the wonderful and good things that you have experienced. It's your brain, and your thoughts you are thinking. And you are the one who is one hundred percent responsible for what you think.

So, think positively rather than negatively. Get those positive juices flowing again rather than sitting in the muck of the sad feelings that are keeping you blue.

Another terrific way to quickly getting yourself re-centered is to go for a walk in a lush green forest. The color green resonates to your heart chakra and will stimulate all of the physical senses to get you heart-centered again. Do anything you can to get reconnected to Nature, as there's nothing more soothing for a troubled soul than the beauty and magnificence of Mother Nature. You'll soon feel rested, renewed and grateful for all of the wonderful people and abundance in your life.

While your emotions are a key aspect to how you experience and live your life, remember that there is an entire 'personal energetic Universe' that makes up who you truly are.

This is one reason why it is more important than ever to disconnect from the negative energy that most living in a modern society today are being constantly bombarded with through the mainstream media.

Between the confusing, conflict-oriented and celebrity-focused media and the horrendously violent and fear provoking television shows, it's amazing that any of us can see our own lives from an objective and clear perspective. If you want to create more positive energy in your life, tune out and turn off the negativity.

Next turn on and tune into the limitless flow of positive energy. If you don't think you have enough time in the day to add one more thing to do, simply replace one TV show a day and meditate every morning to get heart centered and get your entire Chakra system back into alignment.

100%

"Your energetic state of calm and determined resilience to move through life's challenges equates to a resonance of knowing strength and serenity rather than scarcity, fear or fight or flight discordance. It is an absolute necessity in order to create quantum health."

26

Quantum Health

Quantum health starts at an energetic level and it is a direct result of the combined harmonic frequency of your emotional, mental and spiritual vibrational resonance. Therefore, simply thinking that eating and exercising according to current beliefs is all you need to do to be healthy will not be enough to achieve your optimal potential of quantum health.

Your energetic state of calm and determined resilience to move through life's challenges equates to a resonance of knowing strength and serenity rather than scarcity, fear or fight or flight discordance. It is an absolute necessity in order to create quantum health.

This is not about your religious faith and beliefs but all about you knowing that you are connected to your innate divine self, despite what religious beliefs you've been brought up to follow. Believing that you need a middleman to negotiate your evolutionary progress is a system designed for one purpose only; control.

There is divine Truth and wisdom in all world religious foundations however the dogma that has been put in place is something that none of us truly need in order to evolve as a human being.

Knowing Truth is another thing altogether. As when you know who you truly are the facades of control, the fears of damnation, punishment and hell fall away to a renewed connection to the true higher self that is you.

The hierarchy of wisdom within the Universe does not threaten or need to instill great fear in order to control. The wisdom of the Universe is Love and it will soothe your soul back to the center of the truth and true you.

It comforts your mind back to serene calm state. It releases the anxiety and fears to restore you to a safe and secure place. It turns judgment into acceptance. It converts conflicts into compassion. And it will lead you step by step back to your Heart where all Truth and wisdom reside.

Because your emotions are magnetic in nature, they are the tour de force of your achieving quantum health. Not only do their magnetic energy powerfully attract experiences to you, they are also chemical and hormonal triggers at the biological level.

Stress activates the release of cortisol – the fight or flight hormone. Too much cortisol contributes to heart disease, diabetes, depression, Alzheimer's, obesity, gastrointestinal problems and weakens the immune system – and much more.

Therefore, getting your emotions under control will go a long way to creating optimal health. Both Yoga and daily meditation are great ways to minimize stress and counteract the long-term effects of stress.

Your mental state; thoughts and desires are electric in nature. They carry a charge of polarized energy across the entire energetic frequency spectrum. Tune into a horror film and you subject yourself to images eyes should never see, especially if you are trying to live a life of harmony and love.

Watching crime drama TV shows have a similar effect of not only exposing you to ideas, visuals and emotional trauma but pushes your frequency down the energetic scale within seconds.

Those images you've just watched under the pretense of entertainment is, once again, designed with a purpose. And that is to keep as many people as possible in a state of fear and resonating at a low spectrum frequency. The lower the frequency of your vibration the easier it is to control you.

The sheer quantity of horror films, suspense and crime dramas, alien invasions and natural disaster films have increased dramatically over the past ten years. This is not a coincidence but by purposeful design to keep you in check and under the thumb of the fear-based control paradigm.

The same goes true for all of the mindless, idiotic TV shows, news, pornography and the non-stop internet distractions. By the same token, thinking about painful memories, holding on to past hurts or traumas will also keep your vibration on the lower side of the scale.

The mind is like a computer. The subconscious mind is like the software to your hardware. So, what you consistently expose yourself to becomes a software program or more accurately, a new energetic blueprint for your frequency output.

While I'm not suggesting that by watching the violent, sad and traumatic visuals of today's entertainment industry you would choose to play out those dramas in your own life, I am simply pointing out that your mental, emotional and spiritual frequencies will be affected. And not in your or the collective world's highest and best interest.

This is one of those areas where you may want to ask yourself the obvious question of what you are truly getting out of watching these types of film and TV shows. If the answer comes back that you're truly not affected by them, hit the eject button and ask yourself again. Only this time be truly honest with yourself.

There is something missing in your own life that you are replacing with all the drama. It could be old patterns of dramatic exchange that you feel you no longer have outlets for, desires to sit in judgment or and energetic addiction to cortisol and adrenaline peak experiences.

When it comes to experiencing emotions, the mind does not discern between actual experiences that are happening now or from the past. Or visual and sound stimuli in the form of film, TV or photos. The emotional results are similar enough to cause the biological triggers for releasing the hormonal responses and release into the bloodstream. Do this often enough and for long enough and your brain rewires itself with new neuropathways which cause you to crave the same experiences over and over again.

Depression and addictions of every kind can be linked back to the very same process of subjecting yourself to patterns of behavior that trigger emotional reactions that cause biological responses. And the hamster wheel keeps turning until you figure it out or your body forces you off through some kind of crisis.

Overall when it comes to mental fortitude, agility and positivity, you will want to begin taking excellent care of the kinds of energetic foods you are feeding it. Once you cut out the negative media streaming, you'll begin to feel better. Add more and more positive thinking, goals and desires along with some good ol' self-discipline and you will be moving up the frequency scale in no time.

Within the current perceived paradigm of reality, there are some basic ground rules in place. Maintaining the optimal health of our physical bodies is one of them.

While environmental toxins can be a catalyst to activating states of ill health, emotional trauma, anger or long-held resentments are always at the root of any serious or life-threatening health crisis.

All emotions resonate at a specific frequency of vibration and can, if allowed to, get stuck and stored at the cellular level. Replaying old memories of hurt, pain and trauma only serve to retain those memories rather than releasing them.

These stored deposits of low frequency emotions can hold you back in life. They can also be the cause of repetitive self-sabotaging patterns in relationships, career, financial instability and health.

Optimum health therefore starts at the cellular level of no baggage allowed. We all have so called negative or painful experiences throughout our lives and many are never forgotten. The key is to get your emotional response to the memories into the neutral spectrum of frequency where it no longer carries a negative charge to it.

Of course, this will take some work to understand how you can recognize, release and take responsibility for every experience you have, but it can be done.

If you treasure your body as the beautiful temple of life that it is, then the work is well worth it. Just like any new health regimen, starting is the hardest part. Your health is all you have and once it's gone it will be that much harder to regain.

The most important step is the first one and that is the

realization that you are 100% responsible for your mental, emotional and physical state of being. We are all being called to recognize that no one else can maintain optimum health for us now.

In the US, our current medical system is broken. Based on a pharmaceutically-driven education system focused on making billions through treating the body as separate pieces, is the main motivator. The body however is a cohesive system designed to work from a holistic approach rather than independent departments that operate outside of each other.

Slash and burn treatments, FDA-approved pills that cause suicide, cancer, organ damage, strokes and heart attacks are not the result of a medical system designed to restore health.

This is not about the physician's best intentions and dedication to helping people. The majority of doctors chose to be doctors with the very best of intentions. Our current system of health care in the U.S. is the doing of individuals motivated by simply making more and more money with no concern whatsoever as to the numbers of people that die as a direct result. Harsh realities are staring us in the face and this subject is one that really needs to change.

Looking within will always reveal the solutions and there is no greater example than taking back your health. Looking to the outside for the answers will only provide a broken system designed to make more money for the few.

Currently in the US, the number one cause of death is doctor related. Shocking but true, this should be a wake-up call to those who still don't see through the façade.

There is a Universal law that states you must reveal your intentions to the public before implementing it. And while the system is totally corrupt, the greedy people who run it very clearly tell us their true intentions through TV commercials that disclose the ridiculous list of potential life-threatening side effects that the latest drug for your restless legs or eczema could pose.

They are following Universal Law by disclosing the potential harm caused by their prescription pills. This is one area where the increased level of awareness is essential. If you want to live a healthy life you must take your health back into your own hands. When you do, you will be elevating your frequency as a result.

Once you start taking full responsibility for your health, the Universe will support you with the tools and resources needed. And with the internet, there really is no excuse not to be fully informed today about what's good for you and what's not.

There are also countless new healing therapies, nutritional discoveries, energy medicine and holistic practices that you can begin implementing along with a new mind-set of healthier day-to-day ways of living.

No matter your current state of health, you can reverse and restore optimum health. We are energetic beings at the core and some of the best new healing therapies work at the electro-magnetic levels. Using light, sound and vibrational frequencies can reset the body's energy field back to a harmonic resonance and alignment. Be open and hopeful. Do extensive research and draw your own conclusions on how to best move forward to restore your health to its optimum state of vitality.

In addition to a broken health care system, there are some genetic premises that were initially made that now need to be corrected. While the conclusions that we are victims of heredity and our family's predisposed genetic make-up were made over fifty years ago, the new and 'disruptive' science of Epigenetics turns that premise on its head. You and I are not victims of our DNA.

How Our Beliefs Affect Our DNA

Recent scientific studies have shown some truly amazing discoveries in the field of microbiology and cellular control. Cellular biologist Dr. Bruce Lipton, a former University of Wisconsin medical school professor and research scientist, and one of the first scientists to conduct such extra-cellular control studies, found that genes can be turned on and off by environmental signals including, thoughts, feelings and emotions, and here's the amazing part: *from outside the cell.*

Dr. Lipton conducted a series of experiments that revealed that the cell membrane, (the outer layer of a cell), is quite like that of a computer chip, and is also the cell's equivalent of a brain. Although this view conflicts with the widely held scientific dogma that genes control behavior, papers by other researchers have validated his iconoclastic thinking.

Dr. Lipton has also been a pioneer in applying the principles of quantum physics to the field of cellular biology. Traditional cell biology focuses on physical molecules that control biology. Dr. Lipton on the other hand focuses on the mechanisms through which energy in the form of our beliefs can affect our biology, including our genetic code.

In his book published in 2005, titled The Biology of Belief, (available at www.BruceLipton.com), Dr. Lipton summarizes such leading-edge science and explores its implications in our lives.

Dr. Lipton shows that human beings can control gene activity and even rewrite their genes by focusing on their beliefs. These beliefs, whether they are true or false, positive or negative, creative or destructive, exist not only in our minds, but are actually stored at the cellular level.

Dr. Lipton has a great ability to put the complex science of this new field of how our beliefs and cellular biology are intimately connected into easy to understand terms. I highly recommend you read his books and watch his video interviews on You Tube to find out more about this fascinating new field he is pioneering called Epigenetics.

Dr. Lipton has also shown that even our most tightly held beliefs can be changed, which equates to the limitless power we each have to shape our lives in the way we want it to be. And while this statement directly contradicts what our current medical and pharmaceutical industries would have us believe, Dr. Lipton's scientific research is evidential proof that we are not victims of our ancestral DNA coding. We are not hopelessly pre-disposed to the frightening potential of life-threatening disease hanging over our heads and our lives.

Dr. Lipton believes that this newly emerging model of our individual beliefs having a direct effect on our cells, even to the level of our DNA coding, has as much potential to affect our medical and scientific paradigm as the field of quantum mechanics has had on the field of physics.

The fact that Dr. Lipton, among others, have scientifically proven that the energy of our beliefs, our thoughts and our emotions impact our bodies at the cellular level, further supports and provides a clear and scientific explanation for the efficacy of energy medicine, light, sound and vibration healing modalities, alternative and natural health therapies.

Isn't it intriguing to now know that our DNA does not doom us to some previously perceived destiny? Do you feel encouraged knowing more of the truth now? New information always comes along at just the right moment before change starts to happen. Whether it's change you initiate or appears out of nowhere, the point is that when your soul is ready for growth, things start to shift.

Some people may want to make changes in their lives but feel trapped or held back by long-held beliefs they've picked up along the way. Other people stay in what I call the 'in between lives' stage. They want their lives to be different, but they are so afraid or so stuck in their patterns of behavior that they do nothing to actually initiate the changes they truly desire. Each day they get up, unhappy and frustrated with the way they look, feel and live, yet they continue to ceremoniously hope and pray that things will somehow magically change for them.

This is what I also call the 'stability of stagnation' in someone's life. When you perceive that doing the same things every day, and in the same way will somehow give you stability in your life. When you are more comfortable with the daily regimen of the 'what is' while also feeling unhappy and unfulfilled, you are living in a state of stagnation.

This is a life-depleting state of energetic frequency doomed for a downhill slide until one day – one way or another - you no longer live on planet Earth.

For those who embrace change easily, the easiest and fastest route is to work through the Universe's creative process. Imagining your new life, job or home starts with a desire for something better. So, start there. Imagine what you want until it's so ingrained in your mind and heart that you can see it in an instant no matter what you're doing. Remember, your imagination is not something you give up once you grow up.

Get those juicy feelings flowing and experience it at every level as if it's already happening in your life. Keep this up until that dark shadow behind the curtain projecting the old habits, worries and beliefs no longer exists. It really is this simple. Will it be easy? That's up to you and based solely on your ability to discipline yourself on the time you spend visualizing what you truly want.

It's not something that anyone else can do for you. This comes down to personal responsibility for what your life looks like and you are the person who chooses what you think and feel on the inside. And as a direct result, what your life will look like on the outside.

Change really doesn't have to be difficult. If you are someone who is uncomfortable with change, or someone who is holding on for dear life to the status quo of your life, then your best bet is to practice your visualization even more. Equally important will be to get your emotions in line with your vision quests so you can begin to anchor your new life in a solid and substantial way.

As you do so, your brain will begin building those new neuro-pathways and your software will soon become hardware. As your dreams become reality, those thoughts and feelings will be exciting your innate biochemical responses and your new life will begin to emerge around you as a result.

You can make change either easy or hard. But when you really begin to 'get' how to create your life through emotional envisioning, life gets a whole lot easier.

Resistance to change is simply fear of the unknown. If you are someone who is highly resistant to change then I recommend you make a game of it. Get curious. Be playful. Pretend as if you were a child again. Call in your inner child and see what she or he has to say about what you want to do. Or if you're really feeling uncomfortable call on your spirit guides or higher self to guide you. Feeling safe in the midst of change can be a challenge for anyone.

But sometimes life calls us to put on our big girl panties and get on with things. Those things all add up to our life in the end and personally speaking I am not going to get to the end and have regrets.

Let go a little bit more each day of the confines you put yourself through ingrained belief systems, perceived societal demands, religious dogma or political climate.

These are changing and in big ways. This crazy time we're all living in right now is calling on each one of us to change with it. And with all change comes an opportunity for growth within, without and with the world around us.

Implementing a simple daily practice of mindful meditation can remedy daily stress tremendously. The goal is to get quiet and go within to calm the body, mind and spirit. Meditation is not about emptying the mind of all thought – it's impossible to do so.

However, meditation is all about accessing the wisdom within and finding the solutions to all stress-related issues or challenges in your life. The guidance you seek is always available to you during meditative states. I recommend an early morning meditation to get the most out of it. Get quiet for twenty minutes before your busy day begins and you'll see a new life blossom.

Get clear and set your intentions for the day. Ask for clarity when confused. Get inspired about your day and making the difference only you can make. Once you start this daily practice, you will bounce back more quickly from any minor glitches the day throws your way.

Another great addition to decreasing stress and increasing the balance and serenity your life is yoga. Yoga will bring your body, mind and spirit back into balance faster than any other physical practice. If you already practice yoga, you will know what I'm talking about.

Breathwork or simply practicing deep breathing is also a quick and easy way to get back to center. Take three deep breaths anytime you're feeling angry, anxious, fearful or confused and see if you don't feel and immediate improvement in your mood.

Treating yourself to massages is another great way to release the stress that can accumulate in the body. If budgetary restraints don't allow for a massage, then taking a long walk in Nature will accomplish the same results.

Investigate, inquire and use your discernment before implementing any allopathic treatment. If possible always start with the most natural and least invasive treatments as many of the today's prescriptions and even over-the-counter drugs can create new and even more damage than the original issue. Lifestyle changes and natural remedies go a long way to allow the body to do what it knows best what to do, and that is to heal itself. Any disease the body creates it can also heal.

Every health issue can be reversed, and your body restored to a healthy state without the need for adding toxic drugs, synthetic hormones or potentially life-threatening side effects. These types of treatments make no logical sense and at the core do not address the root cause of the problem.

New inventions to ancient healing techniques are emerging as readily available health resources.

Aromatherapy is a simple and inexpensive way to activate higher states of frequency through stimulating biological responses through smell.

Homeopathy is used throughout Europe as a first line of defense and treatment. You'll find a Homeopathy store in practically every Italian town.

Stimulating the body's pressure points through Reflexology, acupressure massage and Acupuncture are other great tools to help relieve stress that can build up along the way.

Using crystal and Gem Therapy is another great tool you can implement in your life. Positioning crystals around the home will elevate the energy in every room. Wearing crystals and natural gemstones will do the same as their electro-magnetic fields resonate through each Chakra. Much like a computer chip, they carry the consciousness of Mother Earth. You can program them to support you in a specific way and receive their maximum energetic support from the inside out.

Nothing nurtures the Soul back to serenity faster than being in Nature, so do your best to spend time there. Grounding yourself to Mother Earth solidifies your connection to her life-giving supportive energy. Her electromagnetic field resonates at the same frequency as does the human body's electromagnetic field.

Together, implementing as many of these natural energetic techniques and practices will go far to restoring and maintaining optimum health and well-being. All while elevating your vibration to higher states of frequency for optimum quantum health.

While science says that 90% of all disease is caused by stress, surely the other 10% is now caused by environmental toxins.

Without belaboring the obvious, making necessary adjustments in the water we drink and the food we eat are on the list if you want to live a healthy and long life. Unfortunately, chemical pesticides, additives, preservatives, food colorings and GMO's are in the bulk of our food supply today.

In California, we have Proposition 65 which requires warning signs to be posted where chemicals known to cause cancer are used. These signs are posted at community and public swimming pools, on store shelves selling lead crystal stemware and in the bakery departments of our grocery stores. One big reason for this is due to the agricultural practice of spraying Glyphosate on grains just prior to harvesting.

But that's not all. According to the EPA, glyphosate is used in production of at least 70 food crops, including a range of fruits, nuts and veggies. It has been found in several types of oatmeal products, including baby food and in several samples of honey.

In case you don't already know, glyphosate is a chemical found in Monsanto's herbicide Round Up weed killer. As recently as February 2018, a federal judge temporarily barred California environmental officials from requiring cancer warnings on food products that contain traces of the herbicide glyphosate.

A March 2015 report by the World Health Organization identified glyphosate as a probable human carcinogen. In addition, some are researching the possible link between the confluence of gastrointestinal issue to this big-agriculture practice. Crohn's disease, celiac, gluten intolerance and others could potentially be avoided by eating organic grains.

Bleaching is another subtle food production practice that does unknown harm on the inside once ingested. Apply logic when it comes to food choices. You would never drink bleach, so why would you eat food that has been bleached white?

Know where your food comes from as well. Ninety percent of garlic is grown in China. While much of it is grown on smaller farms, the peeled variety is especially suspect and although denied by the Chinese officials, smuggled documentary footage shows that it is being peeled by prison labor in highly unsanitary conditions.

Growing practices vary greatly around the world, so do your due diligence before eating anything.

Water as an essential life-sustaining necessity has also become big business. And unfortunately, in some large cities they are adding a new chemical in the water treatment plants due to chlorine evaporating and making it more and more difficult to produce clean drinking water. Investigate your public water supply and treatment to make an informed decision about drinking and cooking with it are in your best interest. There are some great filtration systems that will remove most of the many toxins getting into our public water supplies.

While I'm not a huge fan of bottled water due to the added waste it creates, sometimes it's the best and most affordable solution for clean drinking water. However, be aware that leaving plastic bottles in the hot sun will release Xenoestrogens into the water. Xenoestrogens are a type of xenohormone that imitates estrogen. Synthetic Xenoestrogens are wildly used in industrial compounds such as PCBs, BPA and phthalates. They have been linked to male breast development, obesity, neurobehavioral problems, reproductive abnormalities as well as breast and prostate cancers.

Microwaving food in plastic containers or take out foods in plastic containers also pose the same hazards. There have been many major studies on this subject than can easily be researched in greater depth if you want more details.

Again, due diligence rests with each individual to decide for themselves. But getting informed before you make a choice is the always the best bet and in your highest interest.

This is my short list on environmental triggers to health issue worth looking into. There's great work being done on the solutions and there is always power in the truth when you embrace it.

Personal Care Products – Your skin is your largest waste organ so be wise about what you put on it. Especially chemically based sunscreens. My rule of thumb is to put on your skin only what you can also eat. Unrefined raw coconut oil is my go-to for moisturizing and make up removal.

Know Your PH – Alkaline water is great as long as you truly know what you're drinking. I personally recommend looking into getting a Kangen Water Filter. In addition, cancer cannot exist in a Ph balanced body. High acidic foods, sugar, alcohol, and a heavy protein diet can skew the body's Ph to the acidic side of the Ph scale. You can easily find out your body's Ph by doing a saliva test.

Whole Foods and other natural food stores carry the Ph test strips. If you're on the acidic side, adjust your diet with more alkaline producing foods and decrease high stress levels to get back into balance. You can google alkaline/acidic foods and get informed on what you need to add or delete from your diet to get Ph balanced.

Sugar. We certainly love sugar. I've got a sweet tooth and I know how hard it can be to resist that delectable dessert. Sugar in the US is one of the highest consumed foods, yet probably the worst overall single ingredient to eat. More addictive than cocaine, sugar has become an American diet mainstay and in ever-increasing quantities.

Cancer also thrives on sugar. Whether natural or chemically derived, sugar is something to minimize in your diet. Sugar is also highly inflammatory in the body and is the true cause of high cholesterol, clogged arteries – caused by the inflammation sugar creates, obesity epidemic and a host of auto-immune diseases.

Fat on the other hand is the fuel your body was designed to burn for energy. The right kinds of fats will make all the difference in your brain function and energy levels.

Research ketogenic diets and the healthy types of fat your body truly needs.

Always buy organic, unrefined versions of coconut oil and olive oil. Try buying locally produced options and support your local small producers, not big agriculture, factory farming and corporate size producers.

Goin' Fishing. This is a big subject and full of twists and turns. Never buy farmed fish. Only eat wild caught Salmon and do the research on which fish contain the highest levels of mercury, and other heavy metals. Unfortunately, we're also over fishing the seas and oceans so you may come to the same conclusion I did and that is not to eat much fish anymore.

Taking control of your health is jumping head-first down the rabbit hole. But if you want to live a healthy life today, unfortunately there is really no way around it.

"Following your heart is simply learning to click your ruby slippers together with objectivity to hear the whisper of wisdom point you in the right direction."

27

Your Yellow Brick Road

We all have moments along the way where we reach a crossroads and are unsure of which way to turn. And just like Dorothy, these are the moments when the road before is clouded and you cannot see through the confusion.

The trick is to stop, get quiet and go within. In the end all Dorothy needed to do was click her heels three times and she'd be back home in Kansas. Following your heart is simply learning to click your ruby slippers together with objectivity to hear the whisper of wisdom point you in the right direction. This wisdom comes from your Heart and will always, always tell you what is truly in your highest and best interest.

It may go against logic and what your friends and family may want you to do, but this is your life to live and not theirs.

If you allow your Heart's wisdom to gently lead you through your life, you cannot go astray but will walk the path of your destiny and your Hearts truth to live a passion-filled and purpose-driven life.

The goal is to reach the end of your life and upon reflection not have one regret of something you wanted to do but didn't. Not to have one regret of not loving someone a little bit more.

Not to have spoken the words of forgiveness to those that may have hurt you. Not to say I'm sorry to those that you have hurt. Not to have expressed your Joy a little bit more each day.

Not to have stopped and taken in the vast beauty of the life itself, and the natural world around you. Not to have given back in gratitude for all that you received.

Not to have stopped and made a difference when you knew in your heart that stranger needed a kind word or a helping hand.

Not to have taken more time to listen to your own Heart. Not to have simply lived more, laughed more and loved as much as you could possibly stand.

These are the reasons you chose to be a human being on Planet Earth. You wanted the experiences of feeling the great love and passion for another.

You wanted the experiences of feeling compassion for

another's pain and comforting them in their moment of need. You wanted to be here and feel the feelings that all human beings experience. From the spectrum of fear to love and everything in between.

It is not a fully human experience to sit on the sidelines and not participate. It was not your desire when you planned your next human experience to stay hidden in the shadows of life's adventures and waiting joy.

It was not your Heart's desire to turn away from love and build walls around your heart. It was not your Heart's true desire to disappoint and hurt others.

It was not the true you to act out of spite and revenge, but to stop in the moment and rise above it. The Heart always knows the path it wants to take, it is only for you to stop long enough and listen closely enough to hear the whisper.

This is your time to now rise above all of the past hurts, betrayals, judgment and pain that you have experienced and caused. Throw away the memories and emotions by releasing them to the flames of transmutation. Release these from the grasp that your thinking mind plays over and over and over again.

Release them by writing every last spit of spite, reasoning

for your resentment, harshness for your judgments. Feel every emotion that accompanies these thoughts until you are exhausted with the relief and not one more spec of old emotion resides in your body, mind or spirit.

Now take that piece (or pieces) of paper and burn it while saying the following prayer:

"I release all of my past hurts, resentments and judgments to be transmuted by the Universal Violet Flame. I now go free to love more, live more and to create a path filled with compassion and gratitude for all of my experiences. I now go free to fulfill and live my true Heart's desires and destiny. Thank You. Thank You. Thank You."

The next step in getting back on your yellow brick road and feeling joy in your heart, is to feel, speak and practice Gratitude for everything in your life at this moment. Feeling Gratitude sends out the most powerful energetic blueprint to the Universe for magnetizing more Abundance of every kind into your life.

Every time you think or say: I need, or I want, you are telling the Universe that you are lacking something. That is the energetic blueprint you send out so that is what the Universe will respond with: more lack and more needing.

Every time you get frustrated that something hasn't happened fast enough, you are sending out an energetic blueprint for staying in the feeling of frustration. Every time you feel limited and worry about not having enough money to pay your bills, the Universe will give you exactly what you are telling it you want by giving you a continued experience of lack and scarcity.

You put your request in through not just your thoughts, but with your feelings and the emotions that you express. Your thoughts are the electric component and your emotions are the magnetic component. Together they are the dynamic duo you have at your fingertips to create anything you truly desire. Your emotions are what energize your thoughts and that creates the electro-magnetic blueprint you send out to the Universe.

Now is the time for you to fully understand this power within so you can become the limitless creator you were born to be. This is simply a process of practice makes perfect.

When you sit quietly, open your heart and listen to its whispers of whom you truly are, why you are here now and what you are to do next, then you are stepping on to your destiny path and are ready to begin fulfilling it.

Along with having the courage to taking that first step is to fully understand how to utilize your inner genius to begin to consciously create your life from the heart, one step at time.

This process requires focus, clarity and learning to listen to the wisdom within. Tapping into your heart will transform your life in ways you cannot yet begin to comprehend. And that is where the true adventure of your life begins.

How exciting would it be for you to wake up each and every day and feel the feelings of Joy to be alive?

How great would it feel to wake up each and every morning and know that everything was absolutely perfect in your life?

How beautiful would it feel to wake up each and every morning to and feel the excitement of the new days adventure?

How incredible would it feel to wake up each and every day and know that you were living your greatest passions?

How wonderful would it feel to wake up each and every day and know that you were fulfilling your destiny?

How amazing would it feel to wake each and every

morning and know that you were making a difference in other's lives?

These are just a few of the feelings that you will begin to experience once you open your heart and reconnect with your own Divine Feminine Spirit. Your Goddess within. Your limitless power to create your true hearts desires in any moment you are willing to access and utilize this power.

This is the divinity within each and every one of us. Give this any name that feels right to you. But we are all born with this same divine power and connection to the Universe at large. This is our Divine Creators gift and desire for each one of us to go out into the world and become great limitless creators of our desires and experiences. The world is your oyster. It is only for you to step out of the fear of failure, or rejection, or unworthiness, or whatever you are afraid of and reclaim your inner power and reconnect to your Heart and allow the Divine Feminine Spirit to reemerge in body, mind and Spirit.

This is the time for all people of Earth to step into their mastery and to wear the garment of divinity as limitless creators of vast magnificence. This is the time for all people of Earth to come together and begin to create a new world of harmony, love and peace.

When you allow your life to be driven by your heart, you will no longer be a slave to your mind. The logical mind serves a valuable purpose, but it is the functionary vehicle not the engine that makes the body live a passion-filled life.

Your heart is the center of your Universe and connects you to everyone and everything in the Universe. Your Heart's electromagnetic field is the processor of all of your thoughts, feelings and emotions. It is the superconductor of your life. You must take good care and give it what it needs and protect it from harmful thoughts and emotions that over time will damage it at a cellular level. This is more practice required but will serve you well over the lifetime of experiences and limitless creating.

Once you begin to create from your heart, life becomes much easier. Life's challenges smooth out and you will begin to see the escape clauses built into each challenge or moment of chaos you've created.

Once you begin to master your mind by allowing the heart to take the lead, you will feel a great sense of relief from the fear that once help you captive.

Once you let go of the ingrained belief traps that you have

to do this, or that because it's what your mother wants, or your husband wants, or your friends want, you'll release yourself from the bonds of other's expectations. You will never be happy if you define your life by other's expectations.

There is no power outside of you that can determine your true heart's desires. There is no power outside of you that can tell you how to live your life.

There is no religion, government, school or society that can tell you how to live your life. It is not their life, it is your life. Outside of living with the fundamental guidelines of ethics and moral behavior, there is no power outside of you. You are free in any moment to emancipate yourself from these man-made structures built to entrap you into a system of control and fear. They have no power over you unless you agree to play in their game.

This is the time for you to reclaim your inner power to create from your heart and to stop playing a game of monopoly that only benefits the few. This is your game now and you are the master of it. You are free to set the rules and how to play by them. The people in your life are also free to choose if they want to play in your game. And vice versa.

Regardless of who it is that is presently part of your personal game of life, they willingly choose to play in it. At any moment you are also free to stop playing in someone else's game of life. If you are engaged in a family game that no longer serves you, stop playing.

If you are in a relationship that no longer serves you, stop playing in that game. If you are contributing in a negative way, recognize it and stop the behavior.

Understanding that you are always, and I mean always 100% responsible for your words, actions and emotions is critical to mastering life. In any moment, you have the choice to respond or react to others. This may sound impossible to you now, but I promise you that when you understand that every clash, conflict or confrontation is an opportunity for you to recognize the game and not to engage at the level of your base emotions, you will free yourself from reactionary behavior. It is always an opportunity for growth and personal responsibility to becoming the master of your game of life.

When you find yourself confronted by another the best route to take is one of taking a deep breath. The next is to turn around and take a second breath. Now consciously place an energetic white shield in front of your body. This will break any energetic emotion that will most likely try to hit your Solar Plexus Chakra and cause you to react rather than respond.

Now turn around and face the other person. Feel with your heart before you respond. More often than not, you will see that this is a momentary misunderstanding or miscommunication. Your heart will guide you to the right words to speak and the right actions to take in order to correct the situation.

This is a practice makes perfect opportunity for you to step into the master you are becoming. There is no benefit to anyone involved if you get sucked into their emotions and begin to react with defense, counter-attack or retaliation.

This is why it is so important to begin to understand what belongs to you in the form of energy and what belongs to others. Because your Heart's torus field extends out as far as fifteen feet in every direction, it is important for you to learn how to master your energetic sensibilities.

Understanding that everyone you sit next to, pass by or stand in line behind also has an electromagnetic field emanating from their heart and will go far in helping you begin to know when and why you suddenly feel different.

A great example of this is when you are in line at the grocery store and suddenly you start feeling negative towards the person in front of you. More often than not, this is simply a case of your energetic field picking up on their energy, thoughts and emotions due to your close proximity to each other.

The easiest and best way to avoid these kinds of experiences, which can stay with you, is to always surround and protect yourself with the Divine White Light of Protection.

If you find yourself in one of these moments, consciously draw in your field through conscious intention and place a double bubble of Pink Light around you and the other person.

By the same token, in any emotionally charged situation, you can also send Pink Light to anyone in the moment to discharge the negativity and bring it back into balance through the Universal Frequency of Love.

A wonderful way to use the Pink Light Frequency of Universal Love is when you see any type of accident or conflict between others. Another great way to use this is to surround strangers in it that you see are having a tough time.

Like maybe a mother struggling to calm her toddler having a temper tantrum in a store or any number of other opportunities that commonly come up as we move through our day.

Life affords each and every one of us many choices as we move through it. Each day we wake up with the choice of this being a beautiful and great day filled with limitless opportunities to grow and learn.

Each day we wake up to the choice of being happy or sad. Frustrated or fulfilled. Determined or defeated. Capable or culpable. Successful or a failure. Creative or crushed.

Each morning you can wake up feeling refreshed or tired. But the choice remains a constant every day of your life. There is no other person who can determine or make your day, great, good, bad or indifferent. It is *your* life. No other person can tell you what to think or how to feel.

These are all choices you are responsible for making in every moment of your life. These are choices that determine whether you will take a new step forward on your destiny path to living a fulfilling and passionate life, or a step back into fear, failure and helplessness.

The step back places you in a victim mode of feeling helpless in your life. It makes you feel that you don't know what to do and will suck your energy down into a spiral of self-doubt, limitation and self-pity. These emotions only play one role. And that is to redirect you back into your limitless creator self and the master of your life.

The downward spirals of emotions are warning signs to turn it around and look at the bright side. The downward emotional spiral of playing the victim is a function of getting you back on track and getting you to feel grateful for all of the beautiful friends, family and opportunities that you do have.

The hazard signals of your negative base emotions play an important purpose to turn you back around in the right direction.

If something sad or perceptively 'bad' happens in your life, then the role of feeling all the associated emotions are valid. However, they are not emotions that you want to hold onto, but to move through and then release.

As a human being moving through your life, emotions of every kind will be experienced. The key is not to get stuck in them. Getting stuck in negative emotions will eventually create new neuro-pathways in the brain and physically cause a new program of belief to be played out through more and more negative experiences.

Your thoughts, which cause an electric charge, will activate its corresponding emotional response. When you get stuck in sad experiences or memories that bring you down the emotional spectrum, over and over again, you will begin to create a biological response.

This pattern of repetitive thinking sad thoughts or reliving sad memories will eventually emerge as a state of depression. You have successfully built new neuro-pathways that are activating electrical charges that stimulate the emotional response, which will turn on the biological chemical releases of cortisol – the stress-response hormone. Over time this will deplete your Adrenal glands and leave you tired and energetically depleted.

Over prolonged periods of time, what started as a buildup of reliving the past can develop into serious emotionally based incapacity to fully function in day-to-day life.

Regardless of the names the medical industry gives it, these emotionally imbalanced states are nothing more that old emotions that have created new belief systems with their resulting biological responses. These are all signals that your body, mind and spirit are calling you to attention that something is out of balance and needs taking care of.

How do you resolve any state of depression or sad mood? Even to the point of acute, chronic physical symptoms? Moreover, to the extent of manifesting a life-threatening disease such as cancer, heart disease or any so called autoimmune debilitation?

All acute, chronic and physical dis-ease manifestations are a direct result of a deeply held emotion that has not been released. All disease is caused by some internal state of dis-ease.

All remedies, cures and return to optimum health can be achieved through the process of releasing your hold on past hurt, pain and sadness, whether to the point of hatred for another, contempt or resentment, anger or judgment. All of these deeply held emotions of the negative scale when held onto for long periods of time will eventually manifest at the physical level of life.

This may go against the grain for many, but when you feel this information through the heart, you will see the truth in it. It's not as important that you believe it today, but only to begin processing your emotions rather than holding onto them.

It serves no one for you to live in the past and miss the present. By the same token, it also does not serve you to live in the future with the constant projection of your hopes and wishes for good things to magically appear in your life. There is however true magic in the world when you step in as the master of your life. Good things are said to come to those who wait. There is no question that in order to manifest your dreams and desires that sometimes it also requires patience on your part.

The reason for this is to allow the Universe to do what it does best. And that is to bring all of the right ingredients together in the form of opportunities, synchronicities and people.

And that will always require you to move through the creative process with confidence, faith and fortitude - one step at a time. Your responsibility for stepping into your mastery is to first recognize it. Then the creative process is a simple step-by-step adventure.

- ☐ Move through it with grace.

- ☐ Allow it to move at its own pace.
- ☐ Move toward it with anticipation and excitement.
- ☐ Allow it to manifest in the moment.
- ☐ Move into it with joy and passion.
- ☐ Allow it to become in its own fashion.

This is the magic of life and your ability to create within a limitless Universe with the spectrum of light and love as your palette. Travel your yellow brick road like your life depends on it. Because it does.

"It is time to step into our own Guru shoes."

28

Step into Your Own Guru Shoes

Do you ever think about what Unity Conscious truly means to you in your life? Or in the world? This is a big question to ponder. And I'll bet that most people are not quite ready to take it on and truly explore what this could really mean. Yet, it is something that keeps us all separate, competing and determined to be 'right'.

Some of you will feel that this is a subject best left to the modern-day Gurus. But from my perspective the time has come where it's in our best interest, both individually and collectively, to no longer be a follower of Gurus. It is time to step into our own Guru shoes.

As who knows better than you what is truly best for you? Who knows better what lay within your own heart? What deep desires lay quietly waiting to be expressed?

No one can truly understand another individual's unique perspective, loves lost or pain suffered along the way. All of the fun times, tough times, glad and sad times that make up a very wise soul. And, now it is patiently waiting for you to recognize the wisdom that silently sits within your own beating heart.

This is the Guru of today's exhilarating times in which we find ourselves. Ok, I'll admit that some days appear to be something other than exhilarating. But that's only if you're paying more attention to what's going on outside, rather than what's going on inside of you.

There is this very wise soul who has survived and thrived sometimes too through the years. This wise soul is actually getting ready to make its big debut. This is the time for each bright and shining Heart to wake from a deep slumber and reclaim its rightful place in the world: in your life as your own personal Guru.

But, don't take my word for it. Just make a list of how many times someone else truly knew what was best for you since you've been an adult. If that number is higher than the times you've made the right decision for yourself, then count me wrong.

In the meantime, as each of us reclaims our own inner Guru, the next part falls into place with discovering what Unity Consciousness is all about. As when you step into your new Guru shoes - from the inside out, the need to compete and conquer falls away to a much larger picture, and heart.

"There is nothing more important to do now than experience this sweet spot of being you."

29

Why Now is the Perfect Moment

The practical side to shifting into living moment by moment will take some conscious adjustments and daily practice. One of the most important is to recognize that you can truly only do one thing at a time well. Multitasking is not a desired skill and actually creates stress at every level.

So, begin by doing just one thing, and with your entire focus and energy on that one thing alone. Make a conscious effort to not begin thinking about the next thing, or things that you need to do. Pull your focus back into the moment when you feel yourself starting to make a mental list of all the stuff you still need to do. Realize that thinking about everything you need to do doesn't get it done, it just gets you stressed out.

People are overwhelmed at every level, feeling as though they are running through their day with hardly enough time to breathe. The general feeling is one of resulting emotional stress and mental overload. Multitasking has become an art form for everyday living, yet it only adds to the stress.

And, the mental and emotional stress is taking its toll resulting in physical strain, which can ultimately lead to a breakdown or a health crisis. Life was not intended to be lived racing from moment to moment doing more than one thing, while still thinking of the list or more stuff that needs to get done as you go.

Those of us living in the Western Hemisphere have been living our lives by the calendar since the Gregorian was first introduced. While the clock came later, we've gradually been lead away from living in harmony with Nature's synchronistic schedule and in tune with our interior biological circadian clock we are designed to live by.

Gradually over the centuries, we've become dominated by the importance of what the minute hand says, instead of how Nature works, and we are designed to live.

Now is *the time* to return to living in harmony with the natural world, and this is why we're losing touch with how we used to perceive and experience time in our lives.

Whether you are the type of person who prefers to live for the future or live in the past, your perception of linear time is transforming into the moment. Each one of us is going through the dislodging process of relating to linear time as dictated by clock and calendar. We are remembering how to live in the moment.

When you can make this shift in perception on a conscious level, it will be much like an 'Aha' moment. Your awareness is brought into pinpoint focus, and you will recognize that everything, and I mean absolutely everything is perfect, right here and right now. Everything may not look exactly the way you want it to be, and you will no doubt still have some issues to deal with, but that's called life. We always have stuff we have to handle. That's why we're here and what we came to experience.

Life is meant to be a grand adventure. When you can stop crying over the would'a, could'a, shoulda's, and stop living for the future fantasies that usually have very little to do with what your heart truly desires, you will begin to live in the moment and see your life for the adventure you came here to experience.

Try this quick exercise and see if you don't get a glimpse

of what living in the moment can feel like. Close your eyes and let all of the outer stuff go. Center your attention on your Heart. Now focus your breath and inhale deeply through your nostrils. Then slowly exhale through your mouth. Follow the rhythm of your breath until you slip right into the peace and serenity within.

Say to yourself: "I am here now. I am in this moment and there is no other. Everything is absolutely perfect now. Everything is absolutely perfect in this moment."

You are now in the moment of you and the perfection of being in this moment becomes palpable. There is nothing more important to do now than experience this sweet spot of being you. There is no angst, or stress or friction in the energy around or within you. This will feel like a new experience, yet somehow vaguely familiar. It is what living in the moment is all about and what we are returning to now.

Keep practicing this anytime and anywhere until you feel the sensation of being in the space of the frictionless moment. It's something you will recognize and most likely remember. Practice makes perfect, so start with the most basic of tasks from the moment you get up in the morning. Brush your teeth with the focus of being totally present and you'll do a great job getting those teeth clean.

Once you've achieved getting into this space of the perfect moment with the smallest of tasks, soon you will slip into living your life in the moment, more and more. The more often you get into the moment, you're on your way to living your life in the moment, and in the way, you were intended to experience your life and the world around you.

Adjusting to living in the moment is also affecting many at the physical level. Sleep cycles are swinging between the extremes of sudden physical exhaustion and an abundance of energy. For some people, sound has become something that causes immediate irritation and the need for more quiet time is becoming mandatory. While many people are also waking to an inherent need to eat healthier, and sometimes making drastic changes in their diets to the extent of no longer eating meat.

On the flip side, many individuals are experiencing health issues never experienced before, and doctors are having a hard time identifying the source or treatment. Outside of the obvious conditions caused by poor diet or drug interactions, many more are taking their health back into their own hands, getting off the prescribed medications, and getting healthier than they've been in years.

The shifts on the physical level can be so subtle as to make it hard to put into words; but people everywhere are feeling different and in every way.

Another effect that many people are experiencing is a new attitude of greater compassion and gratitude in your life. Whatever the shifts you are experiencing in your own life, know that while most people aren't openly talking about the changes they are noticing in their own, they are nevertheless happening everywhere, and to everyone on the planet.

"You are here to learn, grow and expand into the greater aspect of who you truly are."

30

The Greater You

To begin living your best life requires a new perspective to the new you. This requires a fundamental plan of action that will take you out of living a stagnant and mediocre life and into the one you've dreamed of living. You are here to learn, grow and expand into the greater aspect of who you truly are.

However, in order to do this, you will need to reconnect and reignite your long held or deeply buried passions for life, certainly for living up to your true potential and fulfilling your life purpose.

Examining your current life state of affairs can often be a difficult process. However long you've turned a blind eye to the realities of your life is behind you now. It's time to get on with things and fix the broken parts and unfulfilled dreams. But unlike Humpty Dumpty, life isn't always a simple puzzle to piece back together. Sometimes you need to wipe the slate clean and start with a fresh palette and brush.

Whatever situation you find yourself in, enter into the new territory of your life's landscape with excitement and anticipation of new adventures to embark upon.

Approach the examination phase with an open mind and heart. Be gentle with yourself. Step out of self-judgment and simply be honest with where you are at now. No crying over spilt milk. Yesterday is gone and the best you can do is to take away the lessons learned and move on.

Get a notebook and pen out. On page one, write down each area of your life. Personal, career, family, love, financial, health and friends. If there are other areas of life you are dealing with currently than this for you, simply add them.

Now on a scale of 1-10 rate each area of your life. As you rate each area, write down these three things for each area as well: I Love these things about my ______etc., I Want More of ______ in my love life, I no longer want ________ to happen or be a part of my life.

Be specific and detailed in the areas that require it. Once you've worked your way through each are of your life, review and add anything that comes up. You may have glimmers of long held resentments and anger that come up in different areas as well. Write these down as they rise to the surface.

Then consciously forgive yourself and those individuals involved in the situation. Then let it go. Say a little prayer to transmute the judgments and emotions through the Violet Flame of Transmutation and return the energy back to Source for purification and release.

The more time you spend on this process of elimination and reflection on the real status of your life, the faster you will manifest your new life. It's a worthy cause so dedicate the time and energy to doing it right and thoroughly the first time around. Leave no hanging participles to come back and tug at your new life. Time to clean out the cobwebs and start fresh.

Once you've completed this process, you should feel a great sense of relief. It should also feel like a fresh breeze just blew in from Spring's sunshine and blooming aromas. If you don't feel a palpable difference on the inside, then go back and review each area again. You've missed something or glazed over an area that you have resistance to looking at honestly. Put the rose-colored glasses away and do the work that your life needs you to do. You'll thank yourself for it later.

You've examined your life in great detail and now know what can stay and what needs to go. You know where you want to fill in some blanks and what you need to move on from.

Experiencing life with a big picture view takes gaining a new perspective for most. It's often not easy to step back and out of the chaos and confusion to see your life with objectivity. It's easy to get caught up in the daily grind and end up mincemeat by the end of the day.

Expansion will be a natural side effect of your creating in a conscious and purposeful way. You will know you are on the right track of your life and expanding when the overarching sense is one of happy anticipation of the new day. You will greet the morning with gratitude in your heart. You will know that what you are reaching for is the right thing for you right now. It will resonate from within.

If you feel resistance and a sense of dis-ease or dread, turn around and review the decisions you made to go this way. More than likely, your mind convinced you that this was the 'right' way to go. Make any necessary adjustments and get back on the right track. Go back and review your cleaning out process. Maybe you have to start over and do it all over again. You've definitely missed something if you are not feeling great about the direction your life is headed in. The key is to feel good from the inside out. Not the other way around.

3

"Wherever you fall on the scale of passions-lived or passions-lost is irrelevant. You are here, and it is now."

31

The Big Three

In order to experience life from a broader view, one needs to reconnect with the 'big three' in life. These three big deals are Love, Passion and Purpose. Without making room for these in your life, you will fail at creating a new life. Without these three elements playing front row to your dreams you will struggle in frustration and confusion.

So, make no mistake, these are the three essential energetic ingredients that are required for every creative recipe, big or small. On an energetic scale, each of these maintains a resonance within the creative frequency spectrum.

Before you jump ahead and start designing your new life blueprint, it's important to better understand the essential energies required to masterfully create in your life.

1. *Love is the Universal frequency for all creation.*

2. *Passion is the energy that propels your desires into the Universe's blueprint.*

3. Purpose is the magnetism that draws your dreams into your manifest reality.

Now on a fresh piece of paper, write down these three things:

Love. Passion. Purpose.

Love.

Start with Love and write down:

Everything you love about your life.

Everyone you love in your life.

What you love most about your life.

What you love about your home, your career, your family and friends.

What you love about life on Earth.

What you love about anything and everything you can think of. Focus only on what you love.

Remember that love truly makes the world go 'round. Open your heart and feel the love that pours into your life from every person, place and flower you see. Feel it. Really feel the love flowing into your Heart from the web of

Universal Love that you and everyone are connected to. Stay in the moment and truly experience what Love really feels like.

The moment will come when your natural response will be how much you love back. Your heart will innately receive and naturally respond with the same. This is how love makes the world go 'round.

Do this exercise and you will never see Love the same way. You will gain a greater grasp on Love's limitless boundaries and unfettered existence through all of life and beyond.

- ☐ Do this right and you will be a changed person for the better.
- ☐ Do this well and you will enter into a state of Bliss and recognize your rightful place in the world.
- ☐ Stay in the moment and you will open your Heart to knowing true Joy again.
- ☐ Open your Heart to the wisdom within and you will remember who you truly are.
- ☐ Accept this knowing and remember why you are here now and what you are to do next.

There is no better feeling and no better place to start your new life than from this place. Dare to go there and you will never look back upon the debris of your life's experiences with more than a fleeting glance. This is the gift that is waiting patiently for you to receive. It is the priceless treasure you've been waiting for. No amount of money can get you close to any of it.

This is the Quiet Revolution of the Heart that each one of us is being called to now. And the world needs it more than ever. You need it more now than ever. Go. Receive. Love.

Passion.

Passion fuels the lives of every person living on Earth. Some experience it from an early age and realize their dreams through a relentless pursuit of achievement. Compromise is not an option. Procrastination is not worth the time you think you will save.

Others hear their passions as a dull roar from within. Resistant to change, many live out their lives watching their passions retreat behind the bars built out of doubt, guilt and fear. And yet others follow in the footsteps of conformity and perceived responsibilities to the point of deathbed regrets.

Wherever you fall on the scale of passions-lived or passions-lost is irrelevant. You are here, and it is now. The fact that you are reading this book means that your soul has called you to wake up and start to smell the roses again.

When you laid out your current life plan, you set certain things in place. You had your game plan organized in such a way that you knew this day would come. No matter the clues or inklings ignored along the way, you've reached your new line in the sand.

And the timing is finally right. Along with many others, your soul designed your life's plan with expertise and impeccable timing. Now is the perfect moment and there's no turning back.

Letting go can be hard. But when you know it's time, it's time. And there is no better time than now to take that leap of faith and jump into the fathom of your deepest held desires. Those passions that have slept while you did what you thought was right. Or you had to do right now.

But they're back. And they are here to stay. Time to put on those big girl panties and get on with the show. It's your life, this you already know. Things are super crazy on Planet Earth right now, this too you already know.

What better time is there than this to create something new and beautiful? Doesn't the world need more beauty? Isn't this a perfect time to make some new music that inspires others? Or maybe to invent a devise or way that makes lives easier? We need your passions now more than ever.

Out of passion comes genius. Genius is the energy of divine inspiration. Ideas to create are the elixirs of life and passion fuels the heart-felt desire to do good in the world.

Passion in its purest form is the wisdom of Universe knocking on your door to do what you came here to do. While receiving a genius idea will come to more than one person at the same time, not everyone will pursue that passion and make something of it.

This is the Universes' way of ensuring that good things will come to fruition. Never one to put all of its eggs in one basket, this insurance plan the Universe has devised usually works out well most of the time.

Now it's your turn. The Universe is knocking on your door. Are you going to answer it or continue to ignore when destiny calls to you?

I will tell you that when you do finally answer to your destiny there's no turning back. It may take some work and maybe longer than you expect at first. But you will have expanded your view of the horizon that lay before you. And it will definitely look different.

Assuming that you put your big girl or boy panties on and have answered the call, the next steps will be necessary to pave the way to the greatest fulfillment you can experience in your lifetime.

On a clean piece of paper write down:

My Passions.

Now write about every kind of passion you have. Whether it's for avocados or to save children's lives. Big or small, all passions have a place in the world. Don't be shy. Write them all down. Dig deep and rediscover those passions long held at bay and let 'em out of the corral.

It's time to let the ponies out and for you to start having some great fun in your life again. Passions are as essential to life as Love. Remember them all. Write them down and see what rises to the surface. You will likely be surprised and definitely not disappointed.

Once you've written them all down, prioritize them. If you could wave a magic wand and live one starting tomorrow which one would it be? Do the same with as many passions as you have. There's no limit here. This is also not about writing your bucket list. This is an actionable passion that you feel a renewed energy to live. It's important. It's of absolute critical importance that you do this now.

Purpose.

This is big. It's the biggest Kahuna of your life. It's what you came here to do. It's what your Soul designed for you in that game plan to fulfill.

At the time you knew it might be a challenge. But remember that you like challenges. You wanted this purpose. You were passionate about your purpose. You'd maybe failed before, but you were committed to not letting anything get in your way this time.

No one would be able to stop you this time. No fears, no doubts, no excuses. This was it. This was your lifetime of getting this right. You knew it. You felt it. You committed yourself to it. And that's why it's coming up now.

At this most critical moment of time in the world. When

humanity is standing at its own crossroads, you said to yourself, you would be one of those willing to stand up and take a chance on change. You knew it could be risky. You knew you could whither in the face of self-doubt and conviction.

You knew others might try to sway you. Convinced it was not your job. Talked out of it by the naysayers. Those well intentioned loved ones who have your back and best interest at heart. No, no you said to yourself. No one, not anything can stand in my way of fulfilling my destiny this time. It won't happen again. It can't happen. Especially now.

This was the level of your conviction when you planned your life's purpose. Are you there? Or are you here? Where do you want to be? Is it time? Or maybe it's something you'll start tomorrow or the next day.

When it comes to reaching this point in your life, there is no more perfect moment than right now. There is no greater gift you can give yourself than stepping onto your life path of fulfilling your purpose. Not to mention that we all really need you to do it too. Not just for us, but for everyone. And the planet. She needs you to do this. Now. It's not too late. Yet.

Beginning to fulfill your purpose takes courage. It also requires commitment. And conviction. And the steadfast determination that no one or anything will stand in your way. Not this time, not ever again.

Take the first step and the second becomes easier. Begin by writing down what purpose those passions you so excitedly wrote down can fill. Step back and see your life from a big picture view. How do you see your place in the world? Where do you see your place in the world? What can you do to make a difference in someone's life today? Tomorrow? The next day and the day after?

What seeds can you plant despite maybe never seeing them sprout? What are you willing to do starting right now that takes you one step closer to your true heart's desires for making a difference in the world?

These are big questions. But only you have the answers. This is where the boys become men and girls become women. Age makes no difference; it's simply about stepping into whom you truly are and why you are here now. Purpose and destiny are the roads that many fear to travel. But this is the time where fear will fall away as quickly as you release your grasp on it. Much like beauty, it is simply in the mind that beholds it.

Your purpose, whether perceived as big or small nevertheless plays its uniquely important role within the times we're all living in. Don't judge it. Grab it by the horns and ride it home. Know that there is nothing more important for you to do than this.

If you are looking for an excuse to escape something you want to avoid, this can be slippery slope. Be authentically honest with yourself. You will feel it at such a deep and knowing level that it cannot be missed. Your purpose will resonate with you in such a way that if allowed to sing its song it cannot be ignored.

If fulfilling your life's purpose is not something you've thought about for a while, or a long time, you may be surprised at your lofty ideals. Don't be swayed. Be illumined by idealistic goals and then go about figuring out how you can make them manifest. It's a starting point of enormous proportions that could make all of the difference in the world. It's not all up to you to see it to fruition just the getting started point.

Once you start, the Universe's job is to bring you the people, resources and support required to see your purposeful goal to fruition. Synchronicity will play a big part. So will your visionary faith and fortitude. No great work is accomplished alone so know that in the beginning while you may feel alone in your quest, it will not remain so for long.

The key will be for you to never give up and never surrender to the challenges you may face along the way. The seeds you plant with your visions, thoughts, feelings, words and deeds all go out and make difference – whether seen by you or not.

This is the true force of the Universe at play. Do not underestimate it. Do not whither in the face of defeat. This will only serve as a point of reflection and necessary adjustment. Sometimes it's simply a matter of gaining a broader perspective. Great things will be happening even though you can't see them yet.

Your passions are reignited, and you have your true heart's purpose in hand and ready for the making. The expansion part comes through the combination of a free fall into your hearts desires and stepping onto your destiny path. Ready to forge ahead in fulfilling your life's purpose you are ready and raring to go.

Remember that the Universe works in mysterious ways. Never doubt it. Especially never doubt your ability to live your purpose. If it weren't possible, your Soul would never have planned it this way.

Breathe.

"With all new life coming into the world, we need to move through the steps before that baby can be born."

32

Push

We are all in a never-before-seen-on-Earth process of evolutionary transformation. It's nothing less than a new life birthing process and we're definitely in the heavy labor stage. It's uncomfortable and at moments painful. Many just want it to be over already. But with all new life coming into the world, we need to move through the steps before that baby can be born.

Some of us are bearing the pain a tad better than others. It just means that we have higher pain thresholds gained by more than likely more lifetimes lived. Not a judgment, just a result of wisdom gained along each individual journey.

Others are kicking and screaming their way through every contraction. This is resistance energy to feeling the crisis stage rather than surrendering to the discomfort of collective change.

However you choose to experience the birthing of a new world process is up to you. Taking deep cleansing breaths in between the hard labor will definitely ease the way.

Keeping your eye on the prize will also ease your way to delivering your new life to the world as well. If you've chosen to birth yourself along with the new Earth, then that is where you are supposed to be by conscious choice.

You are ready. You have worked hard through lifetimes traveled to reach this point in your evolutionary journey. You are embracing Love more each day and can feel its energy lifting you to new heights of creative expression.

This is why you are here now. This is what you came to experience. You chose to live in this chaotic time when there would be so much conflict that it would jar you awake to who you truly are.

Heart in hand and Love embraced you are finally ready to push through the last big contraction and enter your new life and the new world, one beating heart at a time.

That great sense of relief and the beautiful new life you've just given birth to is now yours to nurture. Love it, treasure it and inspire it to live its very best life as the new you. There is no greater gift you can receive. Now go live the greater you that you've worked so hard to become. It is time. It is Love. It is the new you.

Love as a lifestyle

"It is time to see the truth in the lies we've been told. It is time to know our own truths. To know who we truly are. To remember why we chose to be here now. And then to do what we came here to do."

33

It is Time

It is time that we recognize that the chaos surrounding us is evidence of our Hearts no longer accepting of the 'what was'. It is evidence our Hearts are demanding positive change where none has existed for eons. It is evidence the Divine Feminine is rising from within each one of our hearts to say no more.

It is time we hear the voices of oppression. It is time we see the pain of controlled suffering. It is time to recognize the masks of controlled corruption at all pinnacles of modern societies, governments, monarchies, corporations and religious foundations.

It is time to see the truth in the lies we've been told. It is time to know our own truths. To know who we truly are. To remember why we chose to be here now. And then to do what we came here to do. Embracing the Divine Feminine Spirit within each of our hearts will release the power of Love from within, without and the world around us, one person at a time.

It is time to surrender the anger, hurt and damages done for millennia and take up a new dream. A dream of a better life. A dream of a better world. A dream where all people can dream their dream filled with more Love, more Beauty and more Passion than ever seen before on Earth.

It is time to take a stand and recognize our individual responsibilities of giving from our Hearts. It is time to recognize that together we hold the keys to saving our beautiful Earth, and each other.

It is time to release the shackles of fear created to hold us still. To keep us quiet. To repress what is innately within each one of us. And that is the limitless creative power of Love. Love for each other, our lives and all living creatures.

It is time to remember that Love. It is time to embrace that Love. It is time to express that Love in every way, word and deed you express every day.

It is time to restore the power of Love back to Humanity and our Earth. It is time to embrace balance in all things again. It is time to embrace the recognition of our innate divinity and see it in each other's eyes. It is time to embrace the Divine Feminine and the Divine Masculine in each one of us.

It is time to look past our differences and embrace the

beautiful spectrum of our similarities, our diversity, our Humanity. It is time to celebrate the vast creative landscape we live upon and honor our Mother. It is time to do our part in bringing harmony back, from within.

It is time. She's back and there are no returning things to normal. The kind of normal where the few dominate and control the many through fear. The kind of normal where medicine kills rather than heals. The kind of normal where food creates illness rather than maintains health.

The kind of normal where wars are created to fill the coffers of the controllers while filling countless coffins with innocent men, women and children.

The kind of normal where the color of your skin means more than the brilliance of your Heart. The kind of normal where the many are slaves to the few.

It is time that we as a collective Heart now recognize that dreaming for the days to return to normal is a nightmare. It is time that we as a collective Heart rise up into our own Hearts and choose to create a new world. It is time to accept our individual responsibility and recognize that it is the 'we' that agreed to play the game of normal.

It is time now to no longer play that game any longer. It is time to create something greater than normal. Something much more beautiful and loving than normal.

It is our time to say no more normal. We can do much better than normal. Normal is limiting the Hearts capacity to love through a rigged game based on fear. It is our time to choose what we want together.

Choosing to live beyond the bars, bondage and borders of normal releases the limitless creative power of the Universe to live a life based on Love, not fear. A world filled and overflowing with creative expression, innovation and inspiration. A life expressed and lived well with passion, with vitality and with Love.

Choose what you will for each one of us possess the same opportunity to step out of fear and into Love. Now is our time. Alone or together. In fear or in Love. Embrace the status quo of the control paradigms normal life or dare to step into your Hearts limitless potential and dream the dreams that together will create a new world, a new Humanity, and a new life where normal no longer rules the day.

Listen closely to what your Heart is whispering to you now. Pay attention to the clues the Universe is showing you.

And then choose wisely my friend for your and my life depends on whether together we choose to continue on the path of fear or create a new world based on Love.

Let's go there together and create the loudest most colorful, fun and exciting quiet revolution of our Hearts the world has ever seen. It is time for a new renaissance from within, without and with the world around us.

In Love,

Rebecca

?

Epilogue

August 2021

The end to our quiet revolution of the heart is actually just beginning. As the world is in more chaos than ever before, to me the alarm clocks are ringing with bigger and louder wake-up calls than even a few weeks ago.

The frequency of change is escalating and picking up speed like a locomotive out of control. Yet we still have our slumbering brothers and sisters that sleep with their blinders on and ear plugs in.

With each passing day, I feel the winds of change shifting to a more positive stream of great potential. Humanity is stirring. More and more are hearing their alarm clocks go off and are waking up to discovering a world they had no clue they were living in.

This happened to me last year. Despite my ongoing life pursuit in search of the Truth, I too heard my alarm clock go off early last year while on a trip to Florence. What happened over the next sixteen months consisted of extensive rabbit-hole diving that confirmed in the glaring light of day of what I've known for decades.

The facades of the political, media, corporate, pharmaceutical, educational and religious institutions were always transparent to me due to my innate intuition's ability to see the corruption.

With a caveat.

The level of enormous depth and breadth it actually went. It was global in scope and connected at the highest levels.

Power and greed beget the dirty dealings of those who can wield it best. It's a game for those who see themselves above the rest, with a self-righteous entitlement to take whatever they desire, whenever they want. It's a pirate's game rigged out of eons of pure deceit.

Except for one. It was more massive, more beyond human comprehension and heart wrenching than all of the rest combined.

The children.

I will never forget the moment I fully understood what has been going on right under our noses. For decades. I didn't know if I should scream or cry first. It was beyond my comprehension.

Globally speaking, the big picture has come into view, with all the dots connecting, revealing a very dark world I had no idea existed. It largely operates on the surface, and below, yet hidden in plain sight. The entertainment industry showed us through their arm of the elite-ruled underground and they were shoving it right in front of our faces.

Now they are emboldened even more so. See, this is what we're doing. And you can't do anything about it, taunting us to take it all away from them.

It reminds me of the movie a Bug's Life. There's so few of them, these entitled, evil little pirates. Yet there's so many of us.

And guess what they are most afraid of? Those alarm clocks ringing and waking us up. They are most afraid of losing their grip on Humanity through their own rigged game of control through fear.

So, what happens when enough of us wake up and simply stop playing their game? Their game ends. The jig is up, and their house of cards fall on their heads.

We are very, very close. As more bright hearts wake to see

the potential within, there is one less mind controlled by fear machine.

We are reaching a crescendo of alarm clocks ringing. Our hearts are breaking out of their cages and getting ready to fly as any caged bird will do.

Get ready Humanity. For the most exciting, exhilarating ride of your lifetime. It's here and it's happening now.

It's what this time is all about. To open our minds and hearts and step out of the fear and into living love as a lifestyle.

ABOUT THE AUTHOR

Rebecca was born highly intuitive, with a knowing acceptance of all people. She grew up in Wisconsin enjoying a close connection to Nature. At the age of 15, her mother handed her a book on reincarnation that sparked a deep desire within to know the truth about life. This one book opened her mind and heart to ideas outside of the norm.

Over the years, Rebecca studied under three Master Teachers in Los Angeles and New York, fine-tuning her intuitive talents and energetic healing abilities. She began meditating daily and expanded her studies to include The Science of the Subconscious Mind, taught by a Professor at the UCLA Brain Institute, Past Life Regression Therapy, Gem Therapy, Reflexology, the Akashic Records, Western Astrology, Numerology, Feng Shui, Homeopathy, Aromatherapy, and nutritionally-based cleansing and alternative health techniques.

With over forty years of inspiring expertise, Rebecca's innate intuitive and healing abilities, extensive knowledge and combined expertise create a cohesive and unique new system she calls Integrated Energetics. Her WellnessSignature.com site offers an extensive menu of empowering courses, healing techniques and resources.

Rebecca Cherry is also the Author of four books. In addition to The Quiet Revolution of the Heart; a New Renaissance, Rebecca has authored: Follow Your Heart, It's Smarter Than You Think, which explores the true energetic properties of the heart and how it connects you to the entire Universe. Her first book Notes from the Universe, was channeled from the Alpha Centauri who very directly nudge us awake with details of what is really happening now in our world and in our hearts.

Her newest book, Isabella's Earth and the Forces of Doom, is the first of the three-book series, and is a full-length fantasy adventure for children – of all ages. Inspired and written entirely without plot or outline, the book took on a life of its own as the story came to life in her imagination.

The recently launched website IsabellasEarth.com focuses the mission to fully empower and educate children around the globe to help develop sustainable living practices within their homes, schools and communities. This innovative concept for children to create their own community chapters is also a foundation to reconnect children to Nature. A portion of the jewelry sales profits from IsabellasEarth.com will go to supporting children around the world.

Always being artistically inspired to create with her hands, Rebecca launched jewelry design career in 2010 while living in Lucca, Italy. You can find her Gem Therapy Jewelry collections at her jewelry website; www.rebecca-cherry.com.

Her comprehensive work details the true nature of the energetic Universe and how humanity fits and functions within it. She connects the dots from the challenges of today's chaotic world to humanity's transformational crossroads within the Cosmic cycle of change that is upon us.

A Special Note

Once I discovered the horrors of human and child trafficking, I decided to do something about it. I will be donating a portion of my jewelry and book proceeds to helping end this horrific global. Along with supporting children around the globe in whatever way possible.

Please do whatever you can do to help the innocent and vulnerable children of our world. It's up to us as adults capable of making a difference, to do what we are inspired to do.

You can visit my new website; www.isabellasearth.com and buy a bracelet for yourself, a family member or anyone you feel inspired to.

Or get in touch if you would like to get involved in one of the new Isabella's Earth local chapters in your town.

In Love and Gratitude,
Rebecca

Love

Energetic Blueprint Prayers

Here are some simple yet effective energetic blueprint prayers that I use daily. These are to be spoken out loud. Remember that adding the spoken word adds exponentially powerful energy behind them.

Every morning and then again before I go to sleep, I say this prayer of protection. The Divine White Light of Protection will instantaneously and divinely protect you from any potential negative energy impacting your energy field.

You can also say this anytime you feel uneasy or unsafe. I will often times say it again when driving on the freeways – especially after I see someone who is NOT driving safely. Unfortunately, it happens more often than I'd prefer, but at least I include the reckless driver and all of the surrounding drivers in my prayer as well.

Before speaking, take a few deep cleansing breaths to set your focus with clarity.

The Divine White Light of Protection Prayer

"I ask that the Divine White Light of Protection surround and protect myself, (fill in the names of anyone you want to specifically include) _______________, my cats, my dogs, etc, my home, my cars and the vehicles we travel in, all of our family members, our friends and loved ones and see us all home safe and sound, each and every day.

Thank You. Thank You. Thank You."

Healing Energy Prayer

I will use this when my son catches a cold or someone I know needs some healing energy. With every focused intention with added spoken words, you are setting a new healing energetic blueprint.

It will not always work. Sometimes it will work miracles. Sometimes we get sick because our bodies need extra rest in order to be restored. Or the experience is carrying a bigger message to the person who needs to go through the process. Try not to judge or draw conclusions – it's not your job. But there is always positive energy and purpose in feeling compassion for another and sending healing energy. It always helps on some level. Even if you don't see it.

Golden Ray of Healing Energy Prayer

"I ask that the Golden Ray of Healing Energy infuse and permeate every cell of _____________ body, mind and spirt and restore them to perfect health and wellbeing. Thank You. Thank You. Thank You."

New Chakra I AM Blueprint Prayers

I wrote the I AM Prayers to be spoken every day for each area of life. You can use them on specific challenges or adjustments that you are currently focused on improving.

Like all prayers, saying these out loud on a daily basis will elevate your frequency while clearing, balancing and energizing the Chakra center.

Simply saying 'I Am' out loud is a powerful statement of claiming your sovereignty and purpose here on Earth. Adding 'I Am' in front of any positive affirmation, as well as anything negative you may think or say about yourself, also adds a powerful force to the statement you're making.

Therefore, be cautious when saying 'I am…" and choose your words wisely.

To accelerate setting your new Chakra Blueprints, repeat the I AM prayer in the morning and again just before you go to sleep at night. It is important that you say the prayer out loud and with heart-centered feeling.

Repeat daily for forty consecutive days to accelerate your new Chakra Blueprint.

Crown Chakra I AM Prayer

I am connected to my true purpose in life.
I am connected to who I truly am.
I am connected to why I am here now.
I am connected to what I am to do next.

I am connected to my life with passion and purpose.
I am connected to my life with passion and purpose.
I am connected to my life with passion and purpose.

I am grateful for all that I am.
I am grateful for who I truly am.

I am grateful for why I am here now.

I am grateful for what I am to do next.

Thank You. Thank You. Thank You.

Third Eye Chakra I AM Prayer

I am seeing my true purpose in life.

I am seeing who I truly am.

I am seeing why I am here now.

I am seeing what I am to do next.

I am seeing my life with passion and purpose.

I am seeing my life with passion and purpose.

I am seeing my life with passion and purpose.

I am grateful for all that I am.

I am grateful for who I truly am.

I am grateful for why I am here now.

I am grateful for what I am to do next.

Thank You. Thank You. Thank You.

Throat Chakra I AM Prayer

I am expressing my true purpose in life.

I am expressing who I truly am.

I am expressing why I am here now.

I am expressing what I am to do next.

I am expressing my life with passion and purpose.

I am expressing my life with passion and purpose.

I am expressing my life with passion and purpose.

I am grateful for all that I am.

I am grateful for who I truly am.

I am grateful for why I am here now.

I am grateful for what I am to do next.

Thank You. Thank You. Thank You.

Heart Chakra I AM Prayer

I am loving my true purpose in life.

I am loving who I truly am.

I am loving why I am here now.

I am loving what I am to do next.

I am loving my life with passion and purpose.

I am loving my life with passion and purpose.

I am loving my life with passion and purpose.

I am grateful for all that I am.

I am grateful for who I truly am.

I am grateful for why I am here now.

I am grateful for what I am to do next.

Thank You. Thank You. Thank You.

Solar Plexus Chakra I AM Prayer

I am manifesting my true purpose in life.

I am manifesting who I truly am.

I am manifesting why I am here now.

I am manifesting what I am to do next.

I am manifesting my life with passion and purpose.

I am manifesting my life with passion and purpose.

I am manifesting my life with passion and purpose.

I am grateful for all that I am.

I am grateful for who I truly am.

I am grateful for why I am here now.

I am grateful for what I am to do next.

Thank You. Thank You. Thank You.

Sacral Chakra I AM Prayer

I am fulfilling my true purpose in life.

I am fulfilling who I truly am.

I am fulfilling why I am here now.

I am fulfilling what I am to do next.

I am fulfilling my life with passion and purpose.

I am fulfilling my life with passion and purpose.

I am fulfilling my life with passion and purpose.

I am grateful for all that I am.

I am grateful for who I truly am.

I am grateful for why I am here now.

I am grateful for what I am to do next.

Thank You. Thank You. Thank You.

Root Chakra I AM Prayer

I am grounded in my true purpose in life.

I am grounded in who I truly am.

I am grounded in why I am here now.

I am grounded in what I am to do next.

I am grounded in my life with passion and purpose.

I am grounded in my life with passion and purpose.

I am grounded in my life with passion and purpose.

I am grateful for all that I am.

I am grateful for who I truly am.

I am grateful for why I am here now.

I am grateful for what I am to do next.

Thank You. Thank You. Thank You.

Chakra Alignment Prayer

I am aligned to my true purpose in life.

I am aligned to who I truly am.

I am aligned to why I am here now.

I am aligned to what I am to do next.

I am connected to my life with passion and purpose.

I am seeing my life with passion and purpose.

I am expressing my life with passion and purpose.

I am loving my life with passion and purpose.

I am manifesting my life with passion and purpose.

I am fulfilling my life with passion and purpose.

I am grounded to my life with passion and purpose.

I am grateful for all that I am.
I am grateful for who I truly am.
I am grateful for why I am here now.
I am grateful for what I am to do next.
Thank You. Thank You. Thank You.

If you would like to know more about remembering who you truly are, why you are here now and what you are to do next, please visit www.WellnessSignature.com for more information, books, courses, workshops and retreats.

Made in the USA
Monee, IL
27 August 2021

76071042R00184